To Shataun –

I hope you enjoy reading about our daughter's walk with Jesus.

Love,

Denise Bell, M.D.

8-17-19

A Saved Young Life

Now in Heaven:

The Autobiography and Other Chronological Writings
of

Stephanie Bell

Compiled by Denise Bell, M.D.

A Saved Young Life Now in Heaven: The Autobiography and Other Chronological Writings of Stephanie Bell

Stephanie Renée Bell

Contents

Diagnosed with Malignant Brain Tumor June, 2008

Acknowledgments

All praise, honor and glory go to Jesus Christ, our personal Lord and Savior.

We would like to extend our deep appreciation to Senior Pastor Chris Williamson, Family Pastor Daryl Fitzgerald, their wives Dorena and Stephanie, respectively, all other assistant pastors over the years, the elders, all other staff and entire body of Strong Tower Bible Church for their tremendous support during Stephanie's illness and passing into Heaven. The superb nurturing that Stephanie found from the time she first attended the church at the age of 10 years is definite evidence of Christ in action.

Your prayers, home and hospital visits, thoughtful acts of kindness were true blessings to Stephanie and to us.

To all of our friends and family, you have given us unlimited love, discipleship and support in every way; we thank and love you.

We are grateful to the staff of Duke University Medical Center's Preston Robert Tisch Brain Tumor Center, Vanderbilt University Medical Center, Williamson Medical Center and Skyline Medical Center for all of their efforts and accommodations on Stephanie's behalf.

True, deep friendship to a degree that we have never before seen was exhibited by Stephanie's best friends Karyn and Elizabeth, Elizabeth and Karyn (we are saying this both ways because Stephanie and all of us love you equally). Literally there for Stephanie in every way until the very end of her life here on earth, no one could have ever asked for better friends. We thank and love all of Stephanie's friends.

All of our friends and family were sources of tremendous support and comfort, as were friends and relatives of friends and people we never met. It would take an entire book to detail all the kindness shown by so many. We saw the love of Christ shining through you all.

The Bell family

Additionally, I want to express my gratitude and love for my husband William, son Sean and daughter-in-law Lana. In like manner for my son Brandon, whose invaluable technical assistance in the production and publication of this book definitely streamlined the process.
Denise Bell, M.D.

Foreword

"I consider that our present sufferings are not worth comparing with the glory that will be revealed in us."
Romans 8:18

My youngest child, my daughter Stephanie Renée Bell, was on the earth for approximately 654,969,000 seconds, i.e. 20 years, 280 days and 16 hours. At the age of 10 years, she prayed a prayer to accept Jesus Christ into her heart as her Lord and Savior. Total immersion baptism during her teens was her public profession of faith. As a Christian, I **know** that she went to Heaven on March 25, 2010.

"Jesus said to her: I am the resurrection and the life. He who believes in me will live, even though he dies and whoever lives and believes in me will never die."
John 11:25-26

"It's all about Jesus." In November of 2009, during a lucid interval in a hospital room, Stephanie was urgently writing on her blanket with her right index finger. When we gave her a pen and paper to decipher what she was writing, she repeatedly scrawled that sentence, superimposing it on one spot on the paper. That was one of the final sentences and the underlying message of her prolific writing career . . .

In April of 2008, I was reduced for several weeks to sitting in a chair, leaning back; the only position that afforded me relief from continuous, excruciating abdominal pain. This was due to a large liver cyst pressing on my stomach. My appointment with a surgeon specializing in liver disease was weeks away. Surgery was finally scheduled for May of 2008. Stephanie spent the night in a chair in my hospital room the night after my surgery. As time went by I was recovering and requiring less narcotic painkillers. Stephanie had just completed her 1st year at a local community college where she had an "A" average, earning induction into Phi Theta Kappa International Honor Society of the Two-Year College.

On June 1, 2008 Stephanie told me that since her May 17, 2008 birthday she had experienced severe headaches. I took her to the local hospital Emergency Room where an MRI revealed a brain mass. She was transferred to Vanderbilt Medical Center in Nashville, Tennessee, where most of the mass was removed and discovered to be a malignant brain tumor, glioblastoma multiforme. Stephanie later told us that the night before surgery angels came to her in a dream, telling her to do what they said and be very still and they would protect her, not allowing her to awaken during surgery; this had been her fear. The procedure was done June 2, 2008, 1 year to the day after she gave her Middle Tennessee Home Education Association High School Graduation speech.

In July of 2008 my husband William, myself, Stephanie and our 2 sons Sean and Brandon embarked upon the first of numerous over 1100 mile-round road trips Duke University Medical Center in North Carolina where Stephanie enrolled in a clinical trial that was to be administered by them in conjunction with the local medical center, where all of the radiation treatment and most of the intravenous chemotherapy would be given. She also took oral chemotherapy at home. Before heading for home after the first trip to Duke, we went to the coast since Stephanie had never before seen the ocean. We ended up on Carolina Beach on the 4th of July. During a later trip we were sideswiped on Interstate 40 in Knoxville, on the way to an appointment; the window next to my seat shattered; my shoulder was injured; no one else was injured and there was body damage to our vehicle; we continued on to Duke.

Stephanie was unable to attend school during the Fall, 2008 and Winter, 2009 semesters. However, as MRIs and PET scan began to show no evidence of tumor, Stephanie enrolled for the Fall, 2009 semester at the only local university where Speech-Language Pathology (her chosen major) classes were offered at the undergraduate level. She joined the National Student Speech Language and Hearing Association and maintained an "A" average in her coursework and attended classes even when MRIs started to show recurrent tumor and her left arm began to just hang at her side and flail around. She continued to attend until she began to literally stumble and fall.

During that November, 2009 hospitalization she became bedridden. She was discharged to home where we cared for her between ambulance rides, ER visits, further admissions at 3 different hospitals. William and I spent every day and night in her hospital rooms, including the critical care units; Brandon spent most days and nights there. Low blood counts, platelet counts and aggressive tumor growth caused doctors to stop further chemotherapy. Among her requests, I read to her the book of Luke and other Scriptures; her brother Brandon read to her from the book of Ezekiel and other Scriptures. Her brother Sean and many others also read the Bible to her. Our family, church pastors and members as well as other friends held prayer vigils and worship sessions at home and at the various hospitals. The Lord held us up during those times as He does now. Our Strong Tower Bible Church family provided a tremendous level of support. We played nearly continuous music in her hospital rooms. As far as we could tell, God in His infinite mercy spared her from agonizing pain throughout, because after she recovered from the surgery she denied any pain whenever we or her doctors would ask.

On a breakthrough, wonderful day, at Vanderbilt, Stephanie was alert, talking and able to swallow. She began to ask for all kinds of foods. I fed her for hours on end while she ate ravenously. The next day I fed her breakfast but by lunchtime, she was unable to swallow or talk. In the final throes of the disease, her brother Sean asked her how she was doing. She replied, "Good." She was semi-comatose and during her final admission at the local hospital she lapsed into a coma, eventually going to heaven on March 25, 2010. Her faith never wavered.

Stephanie attended a private school until the middle of 1st grade; I homeschooled her through high school, except for 2nd grade, during which she attended another private school. She earned many badges as a Girl Scout and was in the National American Miss Pageant. For many years she was a camper and eventual counselor at a Christian camp promoting unity of all people through Christ.

God supplied Stephanie with multiple gifts. An accomplished classically-trained pianist, she also was a guitarist, music composer (copyrighted instrumentals and lyrics, including Christian rap deliberately written in the vernacular of youth, particularly urban youth, for whom she felt a particular burden), artist and dancer. Some of her music included her pseudonyms "NiteLyte" and "AjiaJade". A petite basketball player with great skills, she played for over 10 seasons in a local community league. She took ballet classes at age 5, stopping because she said it made her neck hurt. When she was older, she attended a church Vacation Bible School and was practicing for a group dance that was to be done during the final day, portraying dancers around the throne of Jesus, but injured her ankle and was unable to be in the final group dance. When we told the nurse at the walk-in clinic the circumstances of the injury, she gave us a card bearing the name of a Christian dance studio. Stephanie subsequently took Christian hip-hop dance classes at that studio, which was owned by that nurse and, along with her brother Brandon, she ministered through dance at local churches, parks, a shopping mall and at the Rescue Mission. Although another injury, a tear of the left knee medial patellar retinaculum in August, 2006 (while doing an exercise routine at home) culminated in open knee surgery and ended her dancing here on earth, she continued to serve as a member and longtime President of the 212 Dance Team of our church where she attended since 1999, becoming a member in 2007. She also served on the church Student Youth Council.

It is, of course, her gift of writing that brings me to this foreword. I have spent much time just trying to find all of her writings and probably still have not found them all. Some were handwritten, others in her computers. Looking back through her home school notebooks I found poetry in spiral notebooks on bound sheets interspersed with bound Chemistry, Biology and Math homework and tests that I had graded. I don't recall seeing this poetry as I was grading the work. She completed 3 novels and started many others. I was aware of the 3 completed novels but only found the poetry and lyrics to her more than

40 songs after she went to Heaven. She also wrote several installments of "fan fiction" as well as many unfinished stories. In her blogs she speaks of her "secret life" of writing.

The fact that many of her *handwritten* works included the date and time of day (of course, the computer writings automatically do) caused me to arrange them chronologically. For those whose date could not be ascertained, I inserted them where the subject seemed to fit with the writings around it. The dates as well as time of day, in my estimation, lend to the poignancy and urgency of her writings, in light of the length of her life on earth. Apparently, oftentimes, she wrote well into the night. As I found more of them, I realized that this compilation was actually autobiographical as well. Her works reflect the degree to which she felt ostracized, especially as a result of the way people, adults and students alike, reacted to her as a home schooled student. As many of the writings were heartbreakingly difficult to read, I procrastinated in collecting them and typing the handwritten ones; not to mention my cataloguing the recordings of her keyboard renditions of her instrumental music compositions and my typing of handwritten song lyrics. Reading her works, however, also provided me with inspiration and comfort, due to the Gospel that she proclaimed. For me, this has been a humbling, incredible journey.

Stephanie touched the lives of many people, including her family, through her ministry of dance, as a camper and camp counselor, and in many other ways. I accepted Jesus Christ as my Lord and Savior after seeing my children on fire for Christ. Stephanie's faith sustained her, supplying strength and courage through a ravaging illness. She walked well in her purpose, which was to glorify God, always acknowledging that her gifts came from Him. She is now perpetually worshipping the Lord, dancing at the foot of the throne of Jesus without limitations. Like the numerous unfinished stories that she wrote, the story of her eternal life will never end.

Stephanie was a gift to us and I thank God for the honor and privilege of being her mother. I'm sure that I did not convey this to her as I should have. These pages are, by far, the most difficult yet joyous that I have ever had to write, their completion facilitated by the guidance of the Holy Spirit. This foreword does not encompass everything that I could say about her. Since her transition to Heaven, the Lord has been holding me up more than I could ever imagine; I am much better than I thought I would be. We more than miss her but we grieve with hope, knowing that we will see her again when we, too, get to Heaven.

In "Abandoned" she writes: "Why am I writing poems that no ear will ever hear?" I could not let that happen.

To God be the Glory,

Denise Bell, M.D.

"In the same way, let your light shine before men, that they may see your good deeds and praise your Father in heaven."

Matthew 5:16

"For we are God's workmanship, created in Christ Jesus to do good works, which God prepared in advance for us to do."

Ephesians 2:10

"We are full of joy even when we suffer. We know that our suffering gives us the strength to go on. The strength to go on produces character. Character produces hope. And hope will never let us down. God has poured His love into our hearts. He did it through the Holy Spirit, whom He has given to us."

Romans 5:3-5

(Note: Stephanie wrote the Romans 5:3-5 quote in a notebook 8-16-06). D.B.

Testimony and Overview

I was in the fifth grade when the Lord called me to accept His Son. Before then, my family's church was located in Ashland City so we didn't go every Sunday. I only went to church on Easter or to attend a funeral. I remember getting dressed up in my Easter dresses every Easter Sunday and my family and I packing into our car to head out on the long drive to Ashland City. We would arrive at the service late, and there was always an Easter egg hunt at the end. I didn't know much about God except that He was kind, loved me, and I didn't have a problem with Him. I was always taught to do right, but I wasn't given a detailed description of the Gospel. I remember how my mom used to read the Bible to my brother and me before we went to bed and my dad used to always tell us to pray when there was a bad storm. I may not have known that salvation was the key to eternal life, but I did know that God was a real person that I should revere and love. I would always say a memorized prayer before I went to bed, (one of those "now I lay me down to sleep" ones). That was as close as I came to God for a while.

But one day when I was about ten years old, my mom, brother and I were coming home from somewhere and mom checked the mailbox before entering our house. She found a green card on it and told my brother and me that it was an invitation to a vacation Bible school being held by our neighbors down the street. It was obviously open to all the kids on my street. At first I didn't want to go because everyone on my street that wasn't a parent or a grandparent was much younger than me, and I didn't want to have anything to do with little kids during the summer. I figured that since I was a fifth-grader, I was better than they were. (And I had always been the type to cherish being older than someone else (I guess that's what happens when you're the youngest in your family)).

But not only did I not want to go because of younger people, but also because I didn't really even know what vacation Bible school was. Mom explained that it was a five-day long seminar on, of course, the Bible. She also told how she had gone to one herself when she was a kid, and how she made different arts and crafts there and had a good time. But still, I wasn't looking forward to it. But whether I wanted to go or not, I went. When getting ready the first day, I was wearing the coolest—as I would put it back then—clothes that I could find just to let the little kids know who was boss. (But I had only just then started dressing more my age, and I figured that fashion was my only solace in that situation). So the first class began. When I walked into my neighbors' yard, I saw that the teacher looked like one of those love-joy hippie-type people and wondered why my mom had done this to my brother and me. I remember her name to this day; it was "Shawna." At the beginning of the class she asked us where our church was and our grade. I spoke very loudly when answering that question and took pride in being a fifth grader. The class continued and I noticed something strange. Shawna was speaking a lot about Jesus. Sure, I knew who He was and all; I just didn't understand why she was talking so much about Him. That is, until we sang a song. It went, "Nothing but the blood of Jesus." And I remember how Shawna spoke of how Jesus cleans us and makes us pure because without Him we're not clean and pure. This puzzled me, but I continued to listen anyway. Shawna finally ended the class by saying that we should accept Jesus into our hearts for salvation. I had never heard that before, or if I had, I was too young to understand. We needed Jesus for salvation? I always thought that everyone had Him in their hearts. Shawna prayed the closing prayer and in it she said an "unbeliever's" prayer for us to repeat in our hearts. Though my head was bowed, I didn't pray that prayer in my heart at that moment. I don't remember why, though.

At the end of each class, there was a time when we'd just have fun and play in my neighbors' yard. Before we dismissed though, Shawna asked all the people who had prayed that prayer to come see her after the class. I knew that I wanted to tell her that I wanted to accept Jesus, but I was too shy and still felt rebellious and closed up to everyone else. But my brother stayed behind and talked with her, though.

I don't remember if it was the last day of the Bible school or the day of the prayer, but while changing my clothes (strange as it sounds) after class, I prayed that prayer as best as I could remember it. It wasn't anything fancy, and I wasn't on my knees with my face on the floor; I just simply asked Jesus to come into my heart and to forgive me for my sins, because even I—as vain as I was—knew that I had done bad things before. And after I prayed that prayer, I didn't feel enlightened or hear voices immediately as you'd think it would be, but just felt a feeling that I'll never forget. It's a feeling I can't explain though I still feel it to this day. The best way I can put it into words, is that I felt someone's presence, as if God were holding my hand or was closer to me than before (because I had always had a sense that someone was watching over me, protecting, and I knew it wasn't just Mom and Dad). And since that day, I've never felt the need to pray that prayer again. Because I believed that that was the day Jesus got a hold on me, never to let go, because He's changed so many things about me, even things that I didn't want to let go of.

But in the end, I've always come out of the change with a smile and praise of thanksgiving, including the change He made back in my room when I prayed the prayer that changed my life.

A big problem I had before I got saved was thinking of myself more highly than I ought. Obviously I wasn't following Luke 14:8 *"When someone invites you to a wedding feast, do not take the place of honor, for a person more distinguished than you may have been invited."*

Later, I received a passion for helping others who are lost, specifically the kind of people Jesus hung out with when He walked the earth. Matthew 21:31, 32: *"I tell you the truth, the tax collectors and the prostitutes are entering the kingdom of God ahead of you. For John came to you to show you the way of righteousness, and you did not believe him, but the tax collectors and the prostitutes did. And even after you saw this, you did not repent and believe."*

Another thing God showed me is that everything I have belongs to Him, and I am his steward. This includes my clothes, money and even my life. James 4:13-15:
"Now listen you who say, 'Today or tomorrow, we will go to this or that city, spend a year there, carry on business and make money. Why you do not even know what will happen tomorrow. What is your life? You are a mist that appears for a little while and then vanishes. Instead you ought to say, 'If it is the Lord's will, we will live and do this or that.' "

212 Youth Group has taught me through the purity course, retreats and Wednesday night sessions, how important it is for me as a teenager to stay alert and ready for battle in these times—because the enemy is real. 1 Peter 5:8-10 *"Be self-controlled and alert. Your enemy the devil prowls around like a roaring lion, looking for someone to devour. Resist him, standing firm in the faith because you know that your brothers throughout the world are undergoing the same kind of sufferings."*

I got injured in a dance practice at a Vacation Bible School and I prayed that someday, God would let me dance again. (I was unable to dance in the VBS finale/production night). My passion is expression, communication of God's gift of art through music, dance, writing and lyrics.

Music has been a love of mine for as long as I can remember. I was raised hearing the piano playing in the living room, and I guess I decided one day that I wanted to play as well. One of my earliest memories is sitting on the piano bench and banging on the keys, trying my hardest to sound like my mom and brothers. Eventually, I suppose my mom grew tired of this, and began to teach me how to play when I was about three years old. Maybe it's because I started so young, but piano came very easily to me, at first. The basics were simple and fun, and a few years later, when I was about 8, I started taking real lessons with Shuff's music. I learned even more about skill and took lessons from when I was 8 until December of 2005, when I decided I needed a break, after meeting my match with a classical piece called "Fantaisie Impromptu." I learned it and "mastered" it to a degree (speed and accuracy was the key), but it drained me and I needed to back off from the intense, classical songs. In the past few years, I have learned about jazz music, and it's my favorite style to play/build on with a piano. As far as songwriting goes, you could probably say it fell out of the sky. I definitely always thought songwriting was for the extremely creative person, but one day I decided to take my chances. I wrote some pretty . . . interesting songs at first, getting a feel for the art using a Korg X3, I taught myself how to lay down tracks and whatnot—and I'm still learning! My style of music is. . . constantly changing, I would say. I believe that music is merely artistic, aesthetic sound, so my style is pretty much whatever I'm feeling. I've written jazz songs, smooth jazz, classic jazz, rock songs, hip hop, soul, Latin, etc. I mix styles very often. Music is a gift of mine, and I pray that God uses it for His glory. At this time in my life, with college on the horizon, I've decided to take a shot at getting my music public, so we'll see where this goes. Most of all, I'm grateful to God for the ability I have to create music—it's one of my favorite things to do.

It's not always easy for me to pinpoint my niche, because I tend to like all styles of music. But if I were to summarize my sound, it would be a combination of classical, hip hop and jazz. Some of my songs have a dramatic feel; others are upbeat with a continuous groove. I like to change it up, and try new things. Though my songs are instrumental, I write lyrics as well. My plan is to try to get into the business of musical scores, jingles, or writing and producing for other artists. I call myself "NiteLyte," because as a believer in Christ, I shine a light in a dark world. I base this nickname on Matthew 5:16:

"In the same way, let your light shine before men, that they may see your good deeds and praise your Father in heaven."

I believe that I should use my gift of music and artistic expression for God's glory. My music is a gift which I give back to God in return.

(Note: the next writing, "True Reality," is an unfinished partially fictional story.)

D.B.

Another cold, cloudy, rainy, and otherwise depressing day as the blue SUV made its way down the highway, had it not been for the rare opportunities the sun gained to catch a small glimpse of the world through the thick clouds. But did I mind? No. I never did—that is, not until I realized just how much good deprivation of the sun for a few days could do to one's train of thoughts. Not to say that I was against it; just in need of a break from it. Something about the clouds and rain allowed my mind to wander into deep contemplation, sometimes about nothing at all, or just little things. Things like my friends, family, what I'd eaten for dinner the night before. But usually how I would handle the day and its upcoming events. Such as dance class, for instance—it could drive me crazy one moment and excite me another. How would I get through it?

The car suddenly swerved to the right only to straighten itself back into the lane again. My thought train having been interrupted, I glanced up and away from the window.

"A piece of a tire in the lane," Mom mumbled more to herself than anyone else from the driver's seat.

"Mm," I said incoherently to acknowledge her remark, then turned back to the window and placed my chin in my hand.

We were headed to hip-hop dance class then, and I wasn't particularly looking forward to it that day. Mom had my brother, Brandon and me in piano lessons every Tuesday, me in my church youth group dance team on Wednesdays (because of my choosing to join it), Spanish tutor on Mondays and Wednesdays, Christian hip-hop dance class on Monday night, and I hoped to have singing lessons soon. Where did school fit into my schedule, you ask? Well, I was homeschooled. Yes, homeschooled—I did say it.

(Now, before I get started on that, let me fill you in on the extremely long story as to how I ended up being homeschooled (and don't worry, when I say "extremely" I'm exaggerating in this case—make a mental note of that)). I began school at a prominent, super-preppy, private school. My parents definitely weren't feeling their true goal. This resulted in them taking Brandon and me out of the school after two years of my being in it, and four years for my brother. It was one of those subjects that wasn't talked about much after it happened, until almost not all as I got older. But, this wasn't the end of my schooling, of course. Next came (yet another) preppy private school but it wasn't as big. It was located in my small, historic town, Franklin, Tennessee. (In contrast to my first school, which was in Nashville.) I was in second grade when I started there and entering third when I left. So, as you can tell, that didn't go too well either.

It was definitely a money and other-students issue. I didn't come from a poor family, but didn't come from a rich one either. So Mom and Dad shifted my brother and me to a new life called "homeschooling." And it was new, alright. It took us years to get used to it. Things went as smoothly as they were going to get what with my Mom (who taught us) away at work until noon and my Dad is usually asleep from being on the road the night before. (My Mom is a doctor and Dad is a truck driver, so driving and medicine were top issues in the family growing up.) But anyway, I had grown pretty much accustomed to my daily routine (which changed consistently from day to day, trust me) and it wasn't really that bad when I didn't let my mind dwell on it for too long. You know how you'll be thinking about something that's bothering or worrying you and it goes from just contemplating the thought to becoming a burden and you're overcome with depression? If so, then that'll give you a good idea of how I felt when I really stopped and considered my situation. But nonetheless, it couldn't be changed, and I had to appreciate what I had, and I did learn to do so. I'll never forget the day when my mom first told me I had to be homeschooled and that that day was my last day at school. I was a little upset over it—sad, I guess. (Now I know I said before how the school was, but back when mom told me the news I was only about six years old and couldn't yet tell one school from another.) It seemed to me like that was the school I'd spend my teen years at and graduate from, so it was hard for me at first, and twice as hard for my parents. They wanted my brother and I to get a good education, and I now understand that.

But back to the homeschooling issue. I'll never forget how different I felt from other people. It was as if the fact that I didn't go to a building filled with kids my age five days a week set me apart from all the rest-made me a misfit. What made it worse was that I didn't realize this until I was about twelve years old—getting into my teens. Before then I would parade around like a normal kid, associating with other kids whether they wanted to be around me or not, and asking them over to my house and to hang out, etc. Little did I know that the majority of them (though nice as they were, don't get me wrong, they were good people) really didn't want to have much anything to do with me. They'd probably accept my friendly invitations and we'd have a good time, but the next week, it was as if they never met me. Only I didn't learn this lesson until my first heartbreak occurred. It started in church youth group—the only place I actually socialized with people my age—and I was crazy over this guy. He had it all going on for him—a drop-dead smile, eyes that could make you stare at him without even realizing it, muscular, nice, sweet, and tall and mature for his age. So I was head-over-heels, only to soon find out that he didn't care about me. One of my friends (one of the only two real ones I had, I should say) asked him whether or not he liked me. He said "No," and claimed that he knew I liked him, because he'd seen a twinkle in my eyes when I looked at him. But crazy as this may sound, that's not what crushed me the most. It was the fact that I was sure I hid my feelings for him pretty well (if I do say so myself) when I was around him, and often caught him staring at me (with that same twinkle in his eyes). So that added an extra twist to the already-tangled web. I finally decided that he found me attractive, but wasn't willing to have a relationship with me, and that's how I've left it ever since. However, even if he *was* helplessly in like with me, he'd have to be a helplessly-in-*love* Romeo that would be willing to wait until I turned about twenty before we could even be seen talking with one another in front of my parents. Now, dating was a whole other story. My parents would have to lose their minds before they allowed me to date a guy while still living in their household. It was an unspoken yet evident law: dating was a forbidden, unholy, unhealthy, unheard-of, and all the other "uns" in the book thing until I was twenty. Nonetheless, I moved on with my life, realizing that it was only one of the natural occurrences of that thing called "growing up," that couldn't be stopped.

So this is where my self-esteem took a violent drop on my roller coaster of life. For about five or six months, I went through the healing phase of my first heartbreak, and came out stronger than when I entered. I was almost fourteen by then, and one of the biggest events to take place in my life was coming up fast. But back to the few innocent months left of being a normal (though abnormal as I may have seemed to myself then) teen. To help me get my problems off my mind I'd write poems, raps, and songs a lot, or play the piano—which had been my main instrument for about eleven years at that point. All my songs were Christian, or Christian-based. That's who I was, and still am. My relationship with Christ was really the only thing that got me through, and I wished that every teen could believe also. If they did, there wouldn't be any trouble in the world, only peace. But that, of course, wasn't going to happen just yet. So I could constantly be found curled up on the loveseat in our living room or in my room writing a song about things that were bothering me, such as youths. Adolescence was one of those subjects that I could go on about forever. If you were to ask me what I thought of the teens of today then, I'd preach the longest sermon ever heard. So many times I'd hear of a young person or friend of mine losing all hope of happiness or joy in life and putting faith into things that don't fulfill their true needs and wants. Too many times I'd hear of one forgetting how to smile. I wanted to reach out to them; to let them know that life doesn't have to be their greatest enemy, but instead a challenge to rise up to and overcome. And I also wanted them to know that I felt their pain too—in different situations, maybe—and just because I'm Christian, didn't mean that I was numb to all pain. I was a teenager too, born to go through the sufferings of adolescence. So songwriting was a good way to vent my feelings; but speaking them out loud and sharing them was even better. I had this dream of being a Christian singer/songwriter/MC. I didn't want anything more than to be on a stage for the rest of my life doing what I loved.

Once when I was thirteen I went to a teen nightclub and competed in an MC battle. It was my first time rapping in front of a lot of people, (and I was extremely nervous because I didn't think that I would actually *start out* on a stage) and it was just like, there I was. No way out, this is what I have to do. I was a nervous wreck but I still had a blast. I made second place against two other guy MCs, so I'm proud of my results. I really believe that if I hadn't gone onto that stage and taken my chance while it was right in front of my face, I would have been disappointed. So that only fanned my flaming desire to entertain. As with a drug, I became addicted to entertaining—from dancing to rapping, or going behind the scenes in a recording studio—I had fallen in love with it. I remember how I used to be in love with basketball—I was obsessed—and how I used to dream of being in professional basketball someday. Obviously, that changed, but basketball still had its place in my heart. But then, dance class came along. It was conceived by a crazy craving that I had to learn how to dance when I was about twelve. So mom finally got me lessons, and from then on I had gained another obsession. At a summer camp I went to, I preferred having dance as my morning specialty over basketball, which was a first. I used to think that I'd never want to do anything but play basketball, but things changed. When I decided that I wanted to dance, I was older, and I think that when you (at an age of more maturity than twelve) make a decision that you plan to follow through on, chances are you're more likely to follow through. But God had many different plans for me. I was just waiting in blindness for something He could make out of my life. I wanted Him to use me for His glory, but for now I just had to wait. I sighed and looked out the window at the vast mountainous region adjacent to the highway. I didn't really feel up to dancing that day; I had low confidence in my dancing a lot of times. *"I'm really tired right now, but I have no other choice but to go to dance class."* But little did I know that that would be my *last* dance class . . .

A Writer Is

A writer is a captain; manning a mighty vessel sailing over waves of adventure
A writer is mist; floating within the shadows and behind the corners of each chapter
A writer is a ghost; haunting those below her
A writer is a counselor; erasing the pain of her patients
A writer is a thorn; stabbing the hearts and fingers of those who touch her
A writer is a rose; her beauty intricately displayed for her reader to behold
A writer is a root; her heart the very depth of the flower atop
A writer is a seed; the beginning of something special
A writer is a kleptomaniac; often unable to refrain from practicing thievery
A writer is an insomniac; sleep is her worst enemy
A writer is a murderer; killing off her creation one by one
A writer is a lifeboat; providing her residents with security
A writer is a slave driver; mercilessly beating her victims
A writer is a mother, willfully giving warmth and grace
A writer is a father; chastening the children with love
A writer is a dreamer; her eyes growing distant at random moments
A writer is a jail warden; closely guarding the inmates
A writer is a prisoner; trapped inside her own work
A writer is a mental patient; she can't let go of her pieces
A writer is a storyteller; relaying an animated tale from the top of her head
A writer is misunderstood; they often call her misunderstood
A writer is a wedding planner; plotting many glorious nuptials
A writer is a lunatic; lost within the pages of her book
A writer is an activist; her cause is always protected
A writer is a genius; for her brain is constantly at work
A writer is vulnerable; she often gets emotional
A writer is a mirror; reflecting every word
A writer is a brick wall; your comments bounce right off of her
A writer is invisible; you'll never see inside of her
A writer is an open book, for everyone to read

When I Grow Up

Create and express
Deliver to bless
"Jack of all trades" is the name I possess
Someday I'll get it—meantime I'm committed
Ask me if I wanna quit and I'll tell ya' "forget it"
It's like Quincy Jones or Debbie Allen
Creative juices pump—accumulate by the gallon
So I gotta release, gotta learn as I go
While I'm followin' Christ, my destiny He will show
Poetry, music, beats and dance
I write from the heart like it's really my last chance
Don't know the chapter, but I know it's my story
And Jesus, the Author, I'll give Him the glory

The Dancer

A stage. A light, shining softly yet certainly, in a room filled with darkness. A broken vase is lying there; the white spotlight surrounding her. She must be waiting for someone because she's alone—visibly trembling at the abyss around her, or is it from something else? She's wearing a white leotard and a long, flowing and ruffled white skirt. Her hair is down freely; she doesn't seem to mind if it gets in her face. The stage floor is black, with a lavender curtain in the background, starlit glitter scattered over its liquid-satin surface. Mysterious, pale azure fog floats from to the sides to the center, where the broken vase is kneeling, waiting for the story to unfold. Her lips are moving; her face concentrated. She must be talking to someone . . . perhaps to the Potter who once created her.

The music begins, coming surely with a quiet over its gently meaningful melody. Her every movement, though once stilled, is transforming into dance; into a state of poetic tale in soulful motion. The vocalist matches the dancer's every move, reflecting what's on her inside; her core. She's singing of not being the kind of girl to fall for anything; about closing her eyes at night and never dreaming. Her moves speak of turning everywhere and finding no one. The stage fills suddenly with blank faces, other dancers who surround her in a menacing circle, these representing the people in her life who seem deaf, mute and blind. She runs to them in a desperate attempt for a solution. . . only to be pushed away. Slowly, the dancer gets to her feet, brushing the dirt off her clean, white skirt. With a sense of hopelessness and despair, she questions if this is the end.

She makes her way to the center of the stage, her hands clasped in fervent appeal, as a different voice comes along, this one clear and compassionate; almost lovingly calming her own cries for help. At the same time, another dancer comes to the stage to personify the voice; this one representing a Potter who never slumbers nor refuses a plea. The second dancer tries to tell the fallen one that she's not alone and that whenever she needed to be fixed, help was there; that the Potter was there and never left. The song softly fades into the bridge, where beautifully graceful dancers come along to witness, their appearance like that of angels. Their words are strong yet gentle, echoing the Potter as they circle the now weeping, doubting dancer. The chorus returns, filled with more power this time, and the lonely dancer's heart begins to soften as the cracks in her clay frame suddenly disappear and turn to a bold and solid, refined gold . . . just what she always wanted.

Father, Son, Holy Ghost, Heavenly Host

Open up your eyes and realize the price is right
I'm required to inspire a generation in the mire, desire to the Sire while the squire
quenches fire,
take it higher
Instrumental madness, consequently sadness
Generation X and all the rest resort to badness
Abstract in the affirmative, intellectual's my relative, spoken word nouns and verbs,
and all merge with the positive, poetic but true, floetic consumed, designated tracks
filled with facts remain intact, reference to the preference of the resident of
repentance, finally they see the light that they were meant to be, filled with
understanding, now demanding what's deep, enemy's prophecy is failure when it's
steep, but my heart still sings for the team with the dream, desire to flip the scene to
see the ancestor's hope of gleam,
But glory seems to cost a price, which is our life, however with head held high they
reach the sky and testify, after they die, their offspring fly and see the aspiration, freedom,
love and kindness while I rewind this to the past, innocent young men
begin to defend, but opponents up the mast, financial temptations commence a war
between nations, ubiquitous warfare still straddles our generations, and seeds of prejudice
and malice are inherited,
Despite the scenario the dilemma remains and fills our veins, but Golgotha held a
bridge to cross into each other's lanes, and now because of sacrifice, freedom is
finally gained.

Runaway

She's just a runaway
'Cause she left herself behind
Just packed her bags and up and went
'Cause she couldn't seem to find
And she's a tear away from crossin' the state line
Tempted to change 'cause they didn't like her name
Not her shoes, not her clothes or the way she talked
Or her lack of finding fame
So she faced the mirror and with a blow she shattered the glass
Then she left the image and grabbed her bags and started running fast
But with one glance back she'll face the fact that He didn't leave *her* behind

1 Corinthians 12:4-7 *"There are different kinds of gifts, but they are all from the same Spirit. There are different ways to serve but the same Lord to serve. And there are different ways that God works through people but the same God. God works in all of us in everything we do. Something of the Spirit can be seen in each person, for the common good."*

Did you know that jealousy and dissension dates back farther than that last argument you had with your best friend over which of you is cuter, more popular, or smarter? The book of 1 Corinthians deals with a whole church being divided by jealousy and quarreling.

The Corinthians were gifted, however they were weak, and didn't understand that God was the supplier of their gifts and the One to be praised for this. They were too busy arguing over who was the greatest and who had the greatest gift. But if all of the gifts came from a fair and loving God, why should they have argued over which is the best? Sometimes you may feel as though your gift(s) isn't as good as the next person's. Well here's a newsflash: the battle you're fighting is a spiritual war, and you'll fight that war until you die. We as humans will always be tempted to compare ourselves with each other—trying to always be "on top," when God loves us all the same and there isn't one thing we can do to cause Him to love us more or less. The "happy ending" is that the war has already been won, and there will come a day when we'll no longer look at each other with thoughts of comparing ourselves, but rather as true brothers and sisters who came to a victory as one, because we are the body of Christ. This means that we are one—nobody is more important to God than another.

Therefore we should live this out—praising God for each other rather than trying to break others down to lift ourselves up, when in truth we're really bringing ourselves *down*. We were given gifts for the edification of each other, which in turn automatically brings *glorification* to God—*not* ourselves.

Give it a Chance

If you knew what it's like, this being a Christian, you'd give it a chance, put first
you have to understand, this love I've found,
Instead of lookin' about you, 'round and 'round

-Chorus-
Let me soar, let me fly, I wanna make it to the sky
With Christ by my side,
I know I can get away

-Verse 1-

A world filled with hate, don't tell me there's no better way
A generation forced to look like all the rest instead of success
Drugs, sex, violence, the trinity of this vicinity, they use drugs to get high, their
own way to the sky
Sex to feel fulfilled, but soon enough will be ill
Violence to vent their fears and hate
Please, Lord tell me there's a better way

-Chorus x 1-

-Verse 2-

To my girls all y'all out tryin' to please the world,
From diet pills to startin' new generations, you're too young, take a contemplation
And on the other station, my fellas hustling the streets, tryin' to flirt and impregnate
every girl you meet,
Tell me why, open your eyes, be a man, be a lady, stop bowin' down to Hades
Look to Christ, He'll guide your life, cover you when you're cold, you can reach
high goals, dig up your childhood dreams
'Cause Christianity is more than it seems,
See we're not a religion, we're a relationship, together we're sons and daughters,
waitin' for our King,
So if you wanna ride wit' Christ, let me hear you sing

A Better Way

Understand me when I say that there is a better way

-Chorus-

There is a better way,
Don't let your troubles take control of all you do
He cares so much for you
So come on get back up, though you think you've had enough
You can do anything, He's there right by your side
All you need to do is open your eyes and realize there is a better way

-Verse 1-

So many people passin' me by, the lost souls, in need of life,
sometimes it makes me wanna cry,
Every kid with a lifelong dream that seems like it won't come true, but,
When I look up to the sky again, I remember God's master plan, can't ya' see He
cares for you,
Just open your eyes and realize that there is a better way

-Chorus-

-Verse 2-

Don't even try it, don't tell me that there's no reason for you to live,
When Christ would give, His very life for you
He made a sacrifice, hear me explain that he's made a sacrifice,
Hear me explain that He's been through pain, He dealt with issues just like yours,
Can't you see that He has high hopes for you, got a high standard for ya' set too,
All ya' gotta do is put ya' life in His hands, and you will be able to smile again . . . 'Cause
there is a better way

-Chorus x 2-

-Bridge-

You're broken, you're weary, your outlook has changed completely
To fulfill the emptiness overtaking you, you'll do anything
So if you want peace, and eternal joy, lift your heart to the loving King

-Chorus x 3 and fade-

History

-Chorus-

Lookin' at everything surroundin' me and this just ain't the way that it should be
But I was once blind, but now I see, that JC's blood's gonna make us free

-Verse-

God I need You ta guide me, ta hide Your Word deep inside me and bide me ta put
You first— not on the side, see
I messed it up so many times I lost count
Yet You still never seemed to let it all amount
It's forgotten
But now my name is remembered, not cold like December but somehow I'm a
member—of the house
You showed me what your love is about
And now I'm gonna shout it like a fire's in my mouth
They might doubt
This love thing goin' down or the chains that had me bound and headed straight to
tha pound
It ain't hard ta see the way You've captured me
I'm gonna let these problems be

-Chorus-

-Verse II-

They tried ta tell me that I was on my own
Tried to sell me and get my mind blown
I should'a known
That there was so much more to their act
Tryin' ta state facts but really a big attack
I step back
And analyze the situation
Satan was always hatin' and tryin' ta be a mate and I was always contemplatin'
Always usin' my head
And didn't understand it was puttin' me ta bed
Spiritually dead
I was walking 'round like a zombie

Like Fitch tryin' ta hold it down without Abercrombie
Guilt trips hit every minute of every day
Seepin' deep inside my soul in every kind of way
I didn't understand what the Word had to say
And I didn't realize that I didn't have ta pay
Pain still remained 'til I leaned back and just rested
It's gone like the Yoda slang: "History the rest is"

Real

Just be real with me, because reality is serious
You can't just take us for granted I know you're hurtin' so share your burdens
But don't let it be from me you're runnin', with God's guidance
I know we can make it
Here's your chance, so please take it,
Don't you know God cares for you, watches what you do
He's real with you
I promise you, so I'll be real with you, too

Look to the Trinity

Verse 1

Began with the phone calls, though was born much earlier
You had a rough day at school; called me up to regain your cool
I listened as always, stayed close by
I always let your angry thoughts fly
Said life was leaving its scar again, said you couldn't pretend
Couldn't front no more
I was your only true friend, who'd be there 'till the end
"Why's life so cruel?" she asked.
I didn't speak up though I had the solution
We were both playin' fools
Sure wish you knew that life hurt me, too

Chorus

Best friends from youth to infinity
Sisters from womb to the tomb
One looks to the Trinity; the other paths that lead to doom
It was black and white unity, our ancestors' aspiration
Differences were erased, but they were forced to face
These truths that would scar and separate them far

Verse 2

One thirteen, the other twelve
Secrets start to surface, they learn about themselves
Truth will set us free, what you would have given to be me
Thought I had it made, thought I was livin'
All 'cause of the gifts I'd been given
The God Man had touched me, opened my eyes so I could see
Thought I got easy love, I had my pass to happiness
While all you got was sadness
She started giving up; she'd had about enough
I carried her burdens, and just the same was hurtin'

Bridge

To all my people who search for truth
Look to the Trinity, 'cause it'll come through
Ya' tried everything to get free, you just gotta see
That all you had to do was look up for your hook up

Chorus x 2

You're the One

You're the One who lets me be me and helps me to see
That you're the only He who would stick around even when there're other fellas
But make me feel wanted because You get jealous and
I need a man to hold my hand, not afraid to take a stand, to show me
He can be my safety and stronger than me
Yet touch me gently, speak eloquently—
And I know
You're the One who won't let me go
Who's unafraid to show who's runnin' this show— so
What can I do but drop my fight
And give you my life
'Cause you paid the price for me . . . So

-Chorus-

You are the song that makes my heart sing
You are the cure for everything
You are my end (end)
You are my start (start)
You are the only one who's holdin' my heart
You are the beat that makes my soul dance
The only One who'd give me a chance
You are my end (end)
You are my start (start)
You are the only One who's holdin' my heart

-Verse 2-

With You I can let my hair down and with you
There's freedom in my sound
All of these gifts You want me to use
But I'ma make sure that I use them for you
'Cause You're the excellence in everything I do
And it ain't hard to see why I owe You my dues—true—
I'm already Yours, sealed by blood
But I've gotta respond to Your love
So I keep my eyes on the sky

I wanna see your face so bad I could die
But until then I'm still gonna try
To live for You and not forget why . . . I'm here

-Chorus-

Other girls said that You weren't enough
But that don't make sense
'Cause You are love
And deep down inside we all need a hug
We all need the One who came from above
I got a love letter
You left me to read
My heart hungers so every day I feed
So I can go out and say to the world
That Jesus Christ cares for men and women, boys and girls

-Chorus x 2 and end-

I want You so bad I got a heart condition
Need You to fix my heart up like a Great Physician
Sometimes it's so much that I can't even write
But I gotta stay focused, gotta stay in the fight
Sometimes it's even hard for me to rhyme
But then again I guess I can't write it every time
-But-
You give me rest when my soul is weary for Ya'

Identity

Is there something you've always wanted to do?
A dream maybe, you've had since the age of two?
Or maybe a quiet voice has been ringing in your soul,
Calling you, beseeching you, wanting you to know,
If you've been wondering how to go with life's flow,
Follow your dreams, hold them tightly, don't let them go,
And even though, someone says you can't make it,
Realize here's your chance, right here and now, you must take it,
When you're let down and no one can be found around,
Remember that quiet voice's sound, now you can face it,
No one can erase it, when the dream's embedded in your spirit,
He designed you to feel it, live it, hear it,
You're name's engraved, you're a freedom slave,
So take the chance, proclaim the truth for the rest of your days,
There's always a way, because He'll make one out of no way,
Remember, don't forget, He's the one that did say
Not to worry, He'll be there in a hurry,
And when you've made it to the storm, trying, surviving, enduring,
Remember He's the only One ensuring,
The storm is nearing, it's low confidence you're fearing,
And now it's arrived, you're striving to survive,
The tears come every single trying day and lonely night,
You're broken, you're tired, no longer inspired,
Used to be outspoken, what's happened to the fire?
But now's the time, the world's so dire,
Get back up, though you think you've had enough,
With Him on your side you can be tough,
Just be careful how you define it, His love is divine it's—
Too great for you to contain it, to the world you must explain it,
Even though you can't quite grasp it, it's no easy task it's—
So hard to endure the scars, but remember that the end of the road is never too far,
He'll provide the rest, though life's not an easy test,
So wipe the tears from your eyes, it's time to come out of your disguise,
The world's telling you lies, can't you see the compromise?
Someone will listen, someone will hear you,
Some are attracted to your essence, because Jesus Christ is near you,
In you, He'll defend you,

Now you're at the top, the height of your aspirations,
Looking back you see all of your anxious contemplations,
But the whole time that voice never died, always at your side, now you realize,
That His love never dies, and who you are in the world's eyes,
Doesn't begin to compare with your identity in Christ . . .

When?

When can I know and believe that you're really looking at me?
When can I stop and see that it's not another, pretty as she may be?
When will I turn around and not be surprised at your eyes I've found?
When will you smile at me and not just any other she?
When can I forsake these games and not be afraid to speak your name?
Will I forever be ashamed or do you really feel the same?
Is there anyone else like you or are you the only one that will do?
And when will I understand that all of this is in God's hands?

Anger

Anger is an emotion that we all can relate to. We let it out when we're sad, annoyed or simply because nothing's going our way. Different people deal with anger in different ways. Some hold it in, which makes it grow more. Others let it out on other people, which only causes more anger to come back directed at you. How would you say you deal with anger?

Anger is something that, when taken out on other people, can spread like a chain reaction. For instance, have you ever heard a rumor about yourself and the first thing you did was react with anger? Though it's an understandable response, it's probably not the best. The Bible says, *"Everyone should be quick to listen, slow to speak, and slow to become angry"* James 1:19.

No matter what method you use to control your anger; your first thought should include God. He already knows when you're going to get angry, and He knows how you're going to handle it. Next time you find yourself getting angry, try to remember that God has an expectation of you, and your desire should be to be more like Jesus. Though we're not exactly called to be perfect, we can still brush up on a few things. Recalling that verse in James when you sense anger arising can help you to better shrug off anger and keep from hurting another person.

The Girl with Incredible Faith
~Dedicated to Twix ~

Growing up the only one of her kind, she had to fight a lot, and sometimes felt as
though losing her mind,
In her heart, the pain would bind, and her enemies would find,
Ways to distress her, even though she was better,
She was made in God's image, and had a promising future,
Satan thought he'd win the war by trying to mute her; breaking her down,
But while he messed around, there was love to be found,
It came through a book, and when she opened it, demons shook,
For they knew it took less than just a look, from Jesus Christ to end their rotten
lives,
In record time, the girl finished the piece, and the blessings descended, providing
her peace,
Mercy said "No" while demons took the final blow,
Though things are still rough, she decides to be tough,
And of Christ's love, she can't get enough,
She'll still find struggles, and trials will come, but she keeps her eyes fixated on
God's Son,
A lesson can be learned from this special girl, and she now holds the power to
face the world,
Don't give up without seeking His face, don't think that your life is erased,
Goodness and mercy will follow those who seek truth,
And to the character of this poem, this is very good news,
So keep your head high, and your eyes to the sky,
Even when you feel you're sinking, God will catch you and you'll get by,
Everything in its season, for your life has reason,
Yes, God can change the world, through one single girl,
For she believed in dark and dreary hours, and trusted in the Lord,
Now she'll hear "Well done" and surely reap reward
A girl with hope; with the decision to do what it takes,
And this is the girl,
With incredible faith

"Just then a woman who had been subject to bleeding for twelve years came up behind Him and touched the edge of his cloak. She had said to herself, 'If I only touch his cloak, I will be healed.' Jesus turned and saw her. 'Take heart daughter,' He said, 'your faith has healed you.' And the woman was healed from that moment."

Matthew   9:20-22

The Sphere

I often find myself crying for what seems like no reason at all
As each tear falls I realize my life can be summed up into a ball
A sphere, complicated and filled with fear, lies, disguise, and no compromise to get
me by
Filled with walls, anxiety and confusion
Anger mixed with sadness constructs my illusion; my outlook on life,
They trail me when I wake and haunt me day and night,
I can live my life in a circle, chasing my own tail,
And when I fall off my horse, my confidence tends to fail,
Rather than dusting off and trying once more, at times I'd rather simply lean against
the closed door
Behind it lies my future, dreams and aspirations,
My eyes fail as tears fall when I make contemplations
I consider my circumstance, and with pride on the exterior I hold my stance
Ready to defend, I pretend I can take the chance
With courage, inspiration and encouragement I ready these weapons of mine
Ambitious "Ajia Jade" then steps up to enemy lines
Running out of time, I ease my mind and lift my gun
It used to be for fun, I say and wish the battle were already won
But little do I know that the war has just begun
Whether hated on, shunned, or accepted, the deal is done
My heart is bound and I've found life is a mere game
You hold on to your dreams, your shooting star, and it seems
We hold onto our fantasies in hopes of better days
While the harsh realities of life steps in with violent ways
Deception of the heart leads to destruction of the soul
Yet we still wish so badly to be able to touch that goal
Our whole lives we wait and hoard life's lessons deep inside
But fear holds us back from those on which we can rely
Friends can't come in because we're taught to defend
So in the end, we end up like a sphere
Constant repetitive travel that only results from fear
The days go by, and we ask why we never tried
To let the walls down and hear the sound of our Tour Guide; the Author of life,
establishing our footsteps in the sand
But we're man, unable to see the difference, or spiritual hopes and dreams

47

Instead we choose to live this life by our own means
Keep your dreams alive and always strive to touch them
Even if it's a mere taste, you'll wait if you love them
Patience is the key to taming your inner feelings
So remember to stand tall with a level head to face that with which you're dealing
The sphere goes on, and though no one feels they belong
We're all more alike than we think, as caged birds singing the same song

Caged Birds

Daily we live, daily we learn
Life leaves its scars, and for love we yearn,
Yet I'm faced with ubiquitous truth in the matter of contradiction
Because we tend to act on fantasies, our dreams are only fiction
So never do we vent, for we're afraid of the consequences,
Afraid to leave the house and cross other neighbors' fences
Afraid to let our baggage be exposed amongst the crowd,
Afraid to drop our pride and let God guide us to living out loud
In childhood we learn to label; youth we learn to judge
Adulthood brings anxiety, and against the innocent there is a grudge
Our lives revolve around the act; keeping our pride intact
And because of this we hurt, and refuse to face the facts
Fear begins to dictate the desires of our hearts,
Like living in a game, we're put right back on "Start"
Dreams can't be reached if our security lines are breached
And since we think we're prospering, incivility is preached
But if you succeed to find a route to the depths of one's soul
You could easily catch a glimpse of the culprit causing this hole
Because though we're constantly faced with feeling we don't belong,
We're more alike than we think, as caged birds singing the same song

The Real Shelter

Sometimes I feel as if I'm drowning,
Drowning in a sea of broken promises and dreams
Gingerly I step into the light, trying to decipher just what it all means
At times I only want to quit the fight, praying for serenity, peace; a state of being
Because now I tend to float, straddling reality and painful abyss
And yet I never would have dared to dream my life would come to this
While I endure and march toward the coveted promised land,
I oftentimes will reminisce on how it all began
"Shelter" became my alias, and eventually my identity
To me they brought their problems, and always would confide in me
Soon enough I felt their pain and knew I'd very well break
The pressure; overwhelming, of much more I could not take
Yet I pushed on, dilemma after dilemma—my sanity at the stake
Now holding on for dear life I try to surface for a breath of air
But just as soon as I see the light, I'm swallowed up before I get there
Losing trust in my own judgments, I carefully choose my friends
Equipping heavy armor with which I can defend
Life is full of years, tears, fears and even hate
We pile the saucer high and can't deny loading the plate
We see the world through rose-colored glasses to satisfy
But never do we realize the real reason why
If I were given one minute to cry out to this land
I'd tell them plain and simple a much better life-plan
Before you decide to only rely on friends and those you trust
Remember there's another being whose opinion is a must
If we could only learn to seek His face first,
The "shelter" as I called her wouldn't feel as if she'd burst.

Dilemma

Where will I put it?
Where can I hide this?
Too many times I've been arrested for my dilemmas
Evidence piling up against me; I'm forced to face the judge
Fictitious stolen position; now a mere human holding a grudge
Why do I search?
Why am I hiding?
I carry a flag dipped in bitter surrender
Acidic dispositions man the reigns of the bandwagon
The fog begins to clear and up ahead lies the dragon
What was I thinking?
What did I do wrong?
The chains hold a little tighter; my burdens far from lighter
Alighting from the vehicle I see the illusion of my destiny
An excruciating porthole to my final resting place
I have to keep the pace; there's no time left for mutiny
When did it happen?
When did I fall?
The noose is tightened and the bag falls over my head
Maniacal laughter echoes from the predators surrounding
I squeeze my eyes shut as my heart starts pounding
In less than a heartbeat I hear the rope slide
At the same time I dare myself to open up my eyes
Darkness envelops me and I search for the pain
Soon enough it hits me—I was spared of being slain
Only dream, I whisper into the shadows
I was spared of my demise, yet my troubles still remain

The Duck They Costumed as a Swan

You call me beautiful
Yet you turn your eyes away from me
You say I'm prized among my peers
Yet never tend to stay with me
You compliment me to my face
But love you won't convey to me
You greet me from afar
But up close you seem ashamed of me
You promise me your attention
When an instant later you hate the sight of me
Describe your darkest hour; the moment you lost your way
Describe to me that second you found out how much life really weighs
What thoughts raced through your mind when you got pushed to the edge?
What did you feel in your broken heart when you finally fell off the ledge?
Relay it as you would to one without feelings
Convey it to the numb in heart and soul; begin revealing
Explain it as a yarn; the plot you hear, feel, and taste
Transmit your inner sentiments, the ones that you embrace
Make them hear you no matter how loud you have to scream
Don't listen to the voices in your head; the two extremes
Simply let your feelings flow as blood dripping from a wound

Spring, 2004

Eternity vs. Popularity

Michael Jensen, 15 years old—Christian? Maybe. Not that it mattered, but his friends often wondered. Popular? Definitely. He could snag any date, any grade, any social status he wanted. One day Michael received a call from one of his friends—Jake Berkeley. They had been friends since the fourth grade, and though they knew each other well, neither had ever really opened to each other. This all changed the moment Jake began to pour his heart out to Michael.

It turns out Jake was a wreck; he confessed to being addicted to pot; his parents were getting a divorce, and he was considering joining a gang. Michael was shocked at his friend's confession. He knew things had been rough for Jake lately with the impending divorce, but he never really thought Jake would break under the pressure.

And then it came . . . a single question that would forever change Michael's life: "What do I do now?" Jake asked.

Surprisingly, Michael knew exactly what Jake needed to do. But would he have the gifts to tell him? Michael had been brought up in a Christian home, went to church every Sunday, and even attended youth group. The problem was, he never could bring himself to witness to others or share with his friends that he was a Christian. It simply wouldn't look right, and he was sure it would ruin his social status. Jake was in trouble, but Michael's popularity would also be in trouble if he were to share his faith to help Jake out—or at least so he thought.

Now, what if the tables were turned and you were Michael? What would you have said? Have you prepared yourself for when a moment like this happens to you? The answer may seem obvious now, but sharing your faith may not always be easy when the time comes. It can be intimidating, even if we teens don't want to admit it. Even Simon Peter, one of Jesus' closest companions, had a hard time claiming Christ the night Jesus was arrested (Matthew 26:31-34).

Matthew 10:32-33 tells us, *"Therefore, whoever confesses Me before men, him I will also confess before My Father who is in heaven. But whoever denies Me before men, him I will also deny before My Father who is in heaven."*

In other words, do not be tempted to do something just because it looks cool or because everyone else is doing it. As Christians, we are to offer our bodies as living sacrifices for God and make a daily effort to die to our worldly desires. Why? Because if we look like the world, we'll eventually be mistaken for someone else—everyone else. And not everyone else will be getting into Heaven. Do you really want to take that chance? I know I don't.

Passion of Christ

He carries the cross as blood drips from his broken, weary body
Burdens he carries willingly for all of the ungodly
With each step He takes He gets closer to that moment
A moment in time where the Master released the binds
Amidst the blood and sweat not a drop of wrong is found
Yet hateful shouts reverberate from an angry swelling crowd
He falls once, twice and I ask when will it end?
So much He must bear to end a cycle known as "sin"
I was taken back in time to a scene of malice and hate
Weapons were prepared before He went to clean the slate
Heartless, coldblooded soldiers hurl insults to The King
How could He endure so much for me—a mere sinful human being?
Mockingly they ready the nails, ignorant that God prevails
With each pound of the hammer I stop and realize I am loved
Not one soul would bear so much so that I could live with Him above
The world goes silent—only laughter from soldiers remain
Clouds fill the once clear sky and His mockers are put to shame
On that eventful day Satan cried like a baby
He cried because He knew from then on Jesus was able to save me
All was finished, all was well, yet my eyes still filled with tears
However, next time I'll think before I say words I'll regret
Next time I'll stop myself before putting off that debt
Next time I'll try a little harder when keeping my thoughts pure
And next time I'll remember what for my sake my God endured

Quote: "I don't know who isn't but I do know that I am; I don't know who does but I do know that I don't." - Ajia Jade (A.K.A. Stephanie)

Play Now, *Pay* Later

There once lived a king who had good looks, victories and the hand of God over his life. However, one day the king found himself sinning because he didn't go off to war as he should have. King David's actions were most likely due to the fact that he was idle—he wasn't working, and probably was bored.

There's something about not being able to find an enjoyable and fulfilling thing to do when work needs to be done that leaves a wide gap for the enemy to step in and wreak havoc. However, that doesn't mean that you have to let him in.

"He who gathers up crops in the summer is a wise son, but he who sleeps during harvest is a disgraceful son." Proverbs 10:5

"Time is of the essence." You've heard it a thousand times. Whether you're a TV addict, internet-aholic, telephone abuser or all of the above—you know you are being idle, but do you know the effects it can have?

Idleness can be found two steps behind many mistakes made by the greatest and smallest of us, and is an issue throughout history. Time cost the great King David his own son, therefore you never know how a few hours of idleness can affect your future.

God will hold us accountable for how we spend our time.

Time is easy to abuse; you've done it, I've done it—everyone has messed up as a result of unnecessary idleness at some point. But did you know that misusing your time means abusing yourself? Think about it, the TV's running, you're kicking back on a lazy day, and as much as you're trying to ignore it, the homework's calling. "Because you're *so* lax and numb to reality, you decide to ignore that little voice (better known as the Holy Spirit) telling you to flip off the set and do your homework, and tune in to that other voice—the one that always seems to have an argument ready for the first one (this argument is usually more appealing to your ears). What's your pick?

"Be self-controlled and alert. Your enemy the devil prowls around like a roaring lion looking for someone to devour." 1 Peter 5:8

The next time you find yourself stuck between work and relaxation, try to look at things with an eternal perspective so that Satan doesn't get the last laugh for the day.

Secret Admirer

Dear beloved,

I adore being around you, so I see you every day
Sometimes you make fun of me,
But I love you anyway
Your smile is beautiful to me; your face like the sun,
But whenever I try to tell you, I end up getting shunned
Your eyes are like diamonds, and often shining with tears
My shoulder is always ready,
But instead you run to peers
You're talented and gifted; blessed in many ways
I wish that you would live only for Me
Because of what I gave
When you look in the mirror, you despise what you see
I love your outward appearance,
Yet you never agree with Me
To me your voice is precious; music to My ears
Yet even better is a song for Me;
And what I'd prefer to hear
When will you understand
That the love you crave is in Me?
My love is unconditional, and I desire you heavily
Why do you run from Me, when I see your every move?
I promise not to betray you,
The way they always do
I shower you with gifts, and devote to you my attention
I fight your battles for you;
Yet you always react with dissension
I love you to the point that your heaviest burden I'd carry
I would even die for you,
So that we could someday marry
I've protected you from age 4, 5, 6 and 7

For you I endured hell, so that you could experience Heaven
I've been with you from the start; I promise to never depart,
And because My love is so strong,
For you I died of a broken heart.

Love,

God

The Keys Called "Love"— Dedicated to Eve

Get up, baby girl, because the door is open
I know the root of everything you're hopin'
I know the mysteries inside your dreams
I know why life is so much harder than it seems
So get up, little child; heart full of desire
I have the rope to pull you out of the mire
You're pleading and bleeding, not looking up above
I can release you, the keys are called "love"
Fall into My love
My arms of peace will catch you
Collapse into My presence
My Word's tranquil as a dove
Lean on my shoulder and let your tears fall
Bask in My strength until you want to give your all
You focus on your pain while I look at your heart
I've been here from the start and promise never to depart
I dare you to give Me your dreams, hopes, goals and aspirations,
Place them in My hands so I can raise them to new stations
For I cannot forsake you, as would an ordinary man
You always fear, and didn't understand
That I cannot forget you, for your heart's in My scarred hands.

My 30th Birthday

My 30th birthday . . . I-I can't believe time passed so quickly. It's funny how all you need is a birthday to get you to stop and think about life . . . God . . . yourself. (laugh lightly and shake head).

That reminds me of something my old youth pastor said once—during a youth group session. And Pastor had a way of making you think—he said that when you stop and be still . . . you think about yourself (shrug). And I guess that's what I'm doing today. There's... so much I messed up on—so many careless mistakes that if I were God I would have taken this unworthy girl out a long time ago (wry laugh). I thank God He's (point up) in control and not me. (Shake head)

I mean, there was so much selfishness . . . (pause and think, frown). We've all been there before . . . but back as a teen— it was like free candy—to take at will. You'd be chillin'— havin' a good time with your friends—you've got your girl on your right—the one that goes back to the sandbox—a few hypocritical believers . . . and that one guy or girl you knew God had been tellin' you to be real with . . . share Christ with . . . (laugh). But not me, right? Psst. Too much earthy stuff at stake to be cursed and laughed at but blessed and rewarded while my Heavenly treasures stock up. God kept speaking . . . and forgiving—His voice, though muffled by my stubborn flesh, kept calling . . . That's mercy to me . . . and it was selfish—what we didn't see was that we had Christ in us; to offer to those who needed His saving power. But if offering the steps for eternal life meant a beating on our "reputations"—it wasn't happening. And what made us look even worse, while showing God's love and grace more, was that He would raise up someone else to be a witness if we wouldn't do it. And that . . . made me mad a lot of times. I felt like God didn't have the right to pass me by like that—like I had done too much—endured too much pain, suffering verbal beatings, tears . . . (shrug and laugh)—might as well have nailed me to a cross and. . . (abrupt stop, blink, frown) crucified me. (sigh).

I missed the fact that I was already dead—dying daily to the desires of my flesh, and that Jesus had already taken the umpteen times worse punishment—for the stupid things I would do some 1,989 years later and beyond . . . for the sin He never nor would ever commit. And somehow . . . I thought I deserved better, when I wasn't even getting the punishment I did deserve. Nothing I went through then or now could match up to what He went through for me. And I still complain. Sometimes I wanted to get closer to my Savior . . . others I wanted nothing to do with Him. The Bible addresses God in so many ways, that we should worship Him . . . as our one and only Idol. I remember thinking about Heaven once, and just how we'll feel about Jesus there. I realized that we're going to want more than anything to be near Him—like starved people hungering for food. I saw that we would go crazy over Jesus like we did for our favorite artists or basketball players, aching to just breathe the air He breathes . . . and eventually I wondered what was keeping us from feeling and living like that then . . . and now.

People were like that in the Bible—on fire for God—kissing His feet and hanging onto His every Word. I guess it was because a lot of them were poor—and they didn't have cable TV, Ciara, 50 or Usher. Jesus was that to them—and much more. But when I was a kid and now even—it's gotten so crazy. If a human "idol" wears this outfit, does this dance, drinks this soda—everybody's gotta do the same, or else you're shot down by what they think about you. What we didn't see was that peer pressure was one of Satan's most favorite toys—weapons of mass destruction to be correct, and bodies of teens who just wanted to be loved and accepted lay in its path.

Too many times I was one of them. I thought I'd go crazy choosing between light and dark—blending in or standing out. One night I spoke with my team leader about this. I told her that I was getting tired, and she told me to remember 1 Timothy 4:12:

"Don't let anyone look down on you because you are young, but set an example for the believers in speech, in life, in love, in faith and in purity."

She stopped me here.

Over time, it made more sense. I, along with a lot of other teens, was trying to blend in with the hungry, when it was my job to give them food, or Jesus Christ's saving power. And truthfully, if I couldn't drop my superficial, selfish pride for one second to look Satan in the eye to say no for a change- to help a friend, most importantly to please God . . . then I had blended in . . . walking in step with a crowd who patted me on the back . . . but while my Idol, faithful friend and true admirer . . . was shedding tears of sadness. Whose feelings would you rather hurt—Satan . . . or Jesus Christ, the One with the hands that are still scarred just for you? I beg you to answer that *now*, not on your 30th birthday.

This World Has Worn Me Out

This world has worn me out, and torn me to bits
With my back against the wall
Is this as hard as it gets?
It doesn't fit—the hurt and the pain
I'm tired of this worryin'— my head hung in shame
In Jesus' name, I find the peace and the glory
All the things I searched for on this building's first story
I didn't find it there, not on Jerry Springer or Maury
I'll only find the love in the death He suffered for me

May, 2005

Sweet 16 Birthday Party Candle Lighting Ceremony

Happiness:

Jessica, thanks for all of the laughs, fun times we had chatting about random stuff, and letting me do your makeup. You are a really sweet person and I'm glad I've gotten to know you. I'm honored to have you be the first person to light a candle on my cake. Please come forward to light the "happiness" candle.

Joy:

Ellen, you know that when we have a conversation, our scheming minds unite to form some kind of crazy plan. I'll never forget our deep talks over coffee and apple cider, both of us growing closer to God, and I can't wait to continue plotting a road trip to surprise our close friend. I would be honored if you would come forward to light the second candle of my cake. Please come forward to light the "joy" candle.

Unity:

Dennis, I remember family get-togethers and parties where you would always light things up. I still remember that basketball game one summer in the backyard, where you showed off your amazing skills. Thanks for being such a great cousin. Would you do me the honor of lighting the third candle of my cake? Please come forward to light the "unity" candle.

Harmony:

Jorie, I always look forward to hanging out with you, and can't forget all of the times we've had. Ever since I can remember I've looked up to you, and love your wit, style and coolness. Thanks for taking time out to laugh, joke and be there for your little cuz'. Please do me the honor of being the fourth person to light my cake. Would you come forward to light the "harmony" candle?

Laughter:

Lauren, I've gotten to know you a lot more in these past few years, and I still can't get over how much we have in common. I admire your fashion sense, heart for God, and easy-going nature. You are most definitely a trendsetter, and I'm grateful to be able to call you my friend. I'm honored to ask you to light the fifth candle of my cake. Please come forward to light the "laughter" candle.

Determination:

Ashley, you have provided such a great example for me and so many others. I remember when you first sat in on a youth group session, and how cool, composed and stylish you seemed (of course, that first impression proved to be true). Your decision to dance for God inspires me to do the same, and I'm grateful for the time you take to teach others, including myself. Your example goes outside of dance, into everyday life, and I thank you for being a strong leader. I would be honored if you would come forth to light the sixth candle on my cake. Please come forward to light the "determination" candle.

Knowledge:

Mrs. Fitzgerald, I'm grateful for your words of wisdom, leadership with the dance ministry, and dedication to the youth group, but I'm also thankful for what you do outside of that. Whether it's reminding me of what's most important, encouraging me with dance, or just setting an example, I am truly grateful. I am honored to have you be the ninth person to light a candle of my cake. Please come forward to light the "knowledge" candle.

Peace:

Brooke, you have done so much for all of the GNC girls, and I'm thanking you especially for all that you have done for me. I'll never forget your willingness to step up and help me, some random girl you didn't even know, when I needed a vocalist for a youth band gig. Apart from that you've inspired me to keep at music, and especially to write songs. Your wisdom has helped me grow, and I'm grateful for the time you take to be there. Please do me the honor of coming forward to be the tenth person to light my cake. Please come forward to light the "peace" candle.

Counsel:

Tammy, at those youth group meetings back at Eagle's Nest, you gave a fresh welcome for me to junior high. I remember one night, way back before the S.H.I.N.E. ministry, where you, me and another girl were in a small group, and how much you really cared about what was bothering us and what we were struggling with. Since S.H.I.N.E., you've only continued to speak life into me, and I'm so grateful for the time you take for that. I am honored to ask you to be the eleventh person to light a candle on my cake. Please come forward to light the "counsel" candle.

Friendship:

Karyn, what more can I say but thank you? You've done so much for me and been there in so many ways. I believe that God made us friends for a reason, and I'll never forget laughing and hanging out with you (just getting to know you) in fifth grade, and I still find it hard to believe that you were once shorter than me. You've always agreed with me and been "on my side" if you will, when it comes to issues closest to me, and things that I struggle with. You are one of the funniest, amazing and wittiest people I know, and never fail to make me laugh. You were there whenever I struggled, a shoulder to cry on when I was away from home, and I am grateful. I pray for many more years to come of this great friendship, and I can honestly picture us still laughing away at "Rhythm & Roots" jokes, your "Yolanda Adams" demo recording, camp or whatever succeeds to still make us laugh 'til our sides hurt when we're old and gray, hardly able to see or maybe even too old dance anymore (if there even is such an age where that's impossible for you). Please do me the honor of being the twelfth person to light my cake. Please come forward to light the "friendship" candle.

Comfort:

Brandon, you taught me all about the basics of fun a kid needs to know. Whether be it playing with Hot Wheels at Nonni & Poppi's, letting me whoop you countless times at Mario Kart (even though you still have me beat at anything else), I can always look to you as being my favorite person to have fun with. I've watched you grow to be a truly godly man of God, with a heart for people and a strong will to do His work. You inspired me to keep my faith, and continue growing. I will always be grateful for the ways you've helped me grow and the times we've laughed. Even though we might sometimes argue, I have to admit that staying angry at you isn't easy. I pray for more years of friendship with you and thank you for everything you've done for me. I love you, and ask that you would do me the honor of being the thirteenth person to light a candle on my cake. Please come forward to light the "comfort" candle.

Discernment:

Sean, I still find it amazing that we have so many of the same tastes, such as music, food and dance, and I am grateful for your example. You too have become a true man of God, and as I am with Brandon, I'm so thankful for your wisdom. I still remember the things you taught me early on, such as dribbling and shooting a basketball, making fried eggs, fried rice, jazz piano techniques, and many more to list. I'm grateful for your dedication to our family. I pray for many more blessings in your life; I love you and thank God for you.

Please do me the honor of being the fourteenth person to light my cake. Please come forward to light the "discernment" candle.

Security:

Dad, you have inspired me in many ways. You've set examples, shown me how to do so many things, encouraged me so much, and taught me about life. I remember how you would turn on our old organ, and play along as I would play on the piano. I remember when I'd sit in your lap and watch TV with you before I was old enough to go to school, all of my brothers' field trips you would have me tagalong to, cutting my waffles for me at the Waffle House, and many more memories that I still cherish. You officially showed me my first dance steps, taught me how to hit a baseball, wash a car, make hot water cornbread, drive a car and countless little things. While doing those things you were spending quality time with me that I'll never forget and will always be grateful for. You taught us kids to be kind to other people, stick with school, love God and so many more things I will hold onto forever. I love you, and am grateful for every single thing you've done for me. Would you please do me the honor of being the fifteenth person to light a candle on my cake. Please come forward to light the "security" candle.

Wisdom:

Mom, I am so grateful for everything you have done for me. You have worked so hard for me, taught me so much, encouraged me and inspired me. I remember trips we would take to Kroger when I was just a toddler, and when you used to teach me before I went to preschool. You are my prime hairdresser, and the time you've spent with me doing just that has gone so much deeper. You too have taught me to be the person I am today, right from wrong in the beginning, how to cook countless things, act in public and many other basic life skills. You've taken me to many basketball games, dance practices, dance lessons, art lessons, school, youth group meetings, field trips, friends' houses, piano lessons, violin lessons—and every other appointment I've had to the point that you've probably driven more miles than the average car tourist. I am so very grateful for that, because I know that if it wasn't for your dedication, I wouldn't be doing any of the things I do today. You were the one who encouraged me not to give up on piano (and wouldn't let me quit), and your strength during times when I struggled with it has kept me going. You've been there and set such a good example for me, providing so much wisdom, and I am thankful for that. I love you and am honored to ask you to be the sixteenth and final person to light a candle on my cake. Please come forward to light the "wisdom" candle.

I Love Psalm 25

I love Psalm 25; it is one of my favorite Psalms if not my favorite—it asks God to take my sins away and remember me; a Psalm that recognizes iniquity and loneliness, and begs God for company as well, acknowledging Him through it all.

Psalm 25 is like the story of my life, speaking many volumes so I read it to survive:

"To you, O LORD, I lift up my soul;
In you I trust, O my God.
Do not let me be put to shame,
Nor let my enemies triumph over me.
No one whose hope is in you
Will ever be put to shame,
But they will be put to shame
Who are treacherous without excuse.
Show me your ways, O LORD, teach me your paths;
Guide me in your truth and teach me,
For you are God my Savior,
And my hope is in you all day long
Remember, O LORD, your great mercy and love
for you are good, O LORD
Good and upright is the LORD;
Therefore he instructs sinners in his ways.
He guides the humble in what is right
and teaches them his way.
All the ways of the LORD are loving and faithful
for those who keep the demands of his covenant.
For the sake of your name, O LORD,
Forgive my iniquity, though it is great.
Who then, is the man that fears the LORD?
He will instruct him in the ways chosen for him.
He will spend his days in prosperity,
And his descendants will inherit the land.
The LORD confides in those who fear him;
He makes his covenant known to them.
My eyes are ever on the LORD,
For only he will release my feet from the snare.
Turn to me and be gracious to me,
For I am lonely and afflicted.

The troubles of my heart have multiplied;
Free me from my anguish.
Look upon my affliction and my distress
And take away all my sins.
See how my enemies have increased
And how fiercely they hate me!
Guard my life and rescue me;
Let me not be put to shame,
For I take refuge in you.
May integrity and uprightness protect me,
Because my hope is in you.
Redeem Israel, O God,
From all their troubles!"

My Side of the Story

Field of Change

I stand alone in a field of change
Noisy silence surrounds me; it echoes my name
Am I to be blamed for my ignorance; should my life rearrange?
But there's nothing I should do— for I'll always be the same
Bales of pain, they cover me, but they are not entirely my own
The prick from a rose belongs to me
Reaping the seed already sown
Someone tried to tell me but I covered up my ears
A prologue of relentless pain wasn't what I'd've liked to hear
Like a child I wanted to cry the teardrops seemingly the size of boulders
But eventually I ceased my search for that understanding shoulder
Somehow, through it all, I recall I have to grow up,
And like a forgotten seed in a field of change, I don't feel that I'm enough

Imprisoned

It returns, it always returns
A lifestyle of looking back—it sears and burns
"Self-sufficient—she's got it together."
Well if this is true then why do I yearn?
Seemingly permanent, but this season will pass
I have to look forward, and not look back
Friends turn to foes, though I promised not to be one of those
I wonder if they see it—the lack in my eyes
My voice, my smile—it's all a disguise
The inside is covered—the real me smothered
The young woman inside—will she be discovered?
I must set her free, for she desires to soar,
Reaching new heights, as never before
But instead she's imprisoned, oppressed by her reflection,
And covering inside of a heart of many complexions

Spoken Word—Eloquent as a Rose

Eloquent as a rose silenced by thorns in the brush
These words travel from heart to mouth in one poetic rush
Art I conceive from a Springtime's eve and Creation's great inspiration
Imprisoned, at first, but now will burst from this mind of contemplation
Directing this pen, the journey begins through a foggy, clouded reflection
Aria unlimited, blood-cleansed, unblemished, but still a heart of many complexions

A Child Can Be Anything

A child can be anything—a doctor, a lawyer or maybe a soldier, a sergeant, a warrior
We watch them play and we watch them grow
But their future is something that we just can't know
I'm sure she watched Him closely when He slept or played outside
But I wonder if she checked to see the future in His eyes
Or maybe in His kindness turned into passion to heal the blindness
Or games of "hide and go seek" that turned into courage to come and find us
People were his passion, so maybe he'd be a politician or maybe a secret agent, bent on accomplishing the mission
His parents had their hopes set high but probably didn't always see
That when asked about the someday Messiah He would reply, "I am He."
Maybe it didn't always line up or fit into their plan
But then again, just how are you supposed to raise the God Man?
Mary told Him many stories and filled His heart with laughter
And all the while He kept preparing her "happily ever after"
Joseph taught Him about life and helped Him learn a trade
But did he know that by his son his life would soon be saved?
So how would you have done it—how would you have raised Him?
Would you give Him orders but then turn around and praise Him?
Would you dream about his future when you already know how it goes?
Though we are centuries ahead, there's clarity in one thing: that without God's help,
None of us could have ever raised the King.

Society's Game

Trying to turn into someone
I'll never be
Aching and crying; the reflection isn't me
But they didn't want the original, they pushed me away
For other, identity's encouraged, but as for me, I cannot stay
So I did the best I could, slipping on the mask
Yet it still wasn't enough for them—this was no easy task
I feel anyone could do it better; anyone would succeed
Yet I run and press toward this goal—the girl I long to be
They look right at me but fail to see the pain that's in my eyes
Or maybe that too is being ignored, and I just now realized
That no matter how hard I try and yearn to win society's game
Their tag on me is destined to be the same and never change

She's a Black Girl

She's a black girl—
She might like Kool-Aid and fried chicken as did those who came before her
She's a black girl—
Potential equal to yours
And a heart that doesn't want you to ignore her
She's a black girl—
She might kick it to hip-hop but in it her tastes aren't confined
She's a black girl—
Music flows through her blood but by it she is not defined
She's a black girl—
Videos, media, clothing aren't truly her tickets to rise
She's a black girl—
Instead of throwing your rock, why don't you step back and look in her eyes?
She's a black girl—
Her momma probably taught her to cook, survive and to dress
She's a black girl—
Not too many generations back she would have been constantly murmuring "yessuh"
She's a black girl—
Fingers trained to style hair and weaves as African queens who came first
Society's dragged through the dirt
She's a black girl—
A royal tradition-turned biggest joke on her-this beauty that's been dragged through the dirt
She's a black girl—
With dreams as high as the sky, aspirations to try and a will trained to put up the fight
She's a black girl—
But not how much skin she can show on reality shows?—don't tell me that this is alright
She's a black girl—
With Barbie doll examples and expectations to be a "10" for her man
She's a black girl—
They say "get as close to white as you can" if her skin is darker and heavily tanned
She's a black girl—
Born as "Laquisha," yeah, she was known as " 'Quisha" as a little girl
She's a black girl—
They say with a name as "black-sounding" as that she won't make it in the real world
She's a black girl—
Her eyes are watching deaths of fathers, husbands, brothers and sons

73

She's a black girl—
Trying to keep with the pace yet erase this cycle that's long-since begun
She's a black girl—
With a culture of music, shame, laughter, tears and pain
She's a black girl—
God has not forgotten her and Jesus can unlock her chains

I Wonder Why

Sometimes I wonder why hearts can be broken
Or why my actions can often be based on my emotions
I wonder why the things I love I turn into things that hurt me
Or why the talent I thought I had now often seems to desert me
I wonder why the passion remains long after the art has departed
So I wonder why this heart for expression ever, ever started

Real or Fake

Real or fake, that's the choice that we make
On a day-to-day basis in the moves we created
Yo' actions speak louder than words can be heard
So if you live for Christ you need to walk out His Word
-and-
Not forget ya' every step is bein' watched, like treasure maps when they x-mark the spot
It's what ya' got, salvation, 'cause time is runnin' out
To tell the whole world what Jesus Christ is all about

I'll Run

Just around the corner; should I go or should I stay?
My heart seems to say it can't be found another way
A little bit ahead and yet so far from my grasp
The scenery is inching by so slow and yet so fast
I know I'm scared to trust, but I want to know what's there
What's hovering deep within the path
This energetic air
I've come and gone so far, and yet it seems it's just begun
Perhaps I'll press on forward—in fact, I think I'll run

"I will run in the path of Your commands, for You have set my heart free"
Psalm 119:32

Creative Juice

What's Your Flavor?

There's a moment, a moment where your hands eagerly hover over the keyboard, waiting for a command from your imagination

Your eyes remain focused on the blank line, subconsciously envisioning words which could fill the emptiness, what symbols will best express your thoughts; tell your story

You close your eyes as your finger strokes a key, the smooth groove in the plastic bringing you back to your senses, though you've never even left them—well, not completely

You take a moment to relax; to let your creativity take you where your story requires you to be

It's your baby, your child—a mute, that cannot speak for itself

As much as people try to tell you to let it "write itself," you are still the voice to be heard, and no one else can write it for you

The desire for excellence causes you to swallow

Anything can compose this next sentence, but anything won't do

You jump at the sound of the air conditioning shutting itself off, and shake your head to stay awake

The slightest noise causes your nerves to jar, for the clock in the right-handed corner of your monitor reads 1:23

You wish it weren't A.M., but know that when the creative juice flows, it must be caught and not wasted—immediately put to work

You rise for a glass of water, tripping over the fallen TV remote as you move across the dimly-lit room

Grumbling as you turn to pick it up, you take notice of the other screen in the room—your TV

A news program is being replayed from the evening hours, and you're a heartbeat away from shutting the set off when a child appears on the screen, burns covering his face and hands

The journalist begins to question him, and silent tears fall down his hopeless face

He was burned in a house fire, most likely by an arsonist, they say

His mother died—his father and baby brother, too

One minute of fame on a news station rarely watched won't wipe the tears

Who has heard his story and cared? How many others have suffered as he has?

You move back to your computer, suddenly feeling inspired. Telling the story of those who cannot tell it themselves has always been the flavor of your creative juice.

Abandoned

Am I unnecessary; the piece that doesn't fit?
Everything I love is destined to hurt me;
Everyone I trust will eventually desert me
Why am I writing poems that no ear will ever hear?
Why do I possess this love for art that only burns and sears?
They're falling off left and right from me, their love continues to slow
The more my trust dissolves in them—I find I'm letting go
My skin is only so thick—I don't think I can take any more
My heart is shattering day by day but they only continue to ignore
What hurts the most is loyalty once displayed to my face
But now that they've left I only see it as mere courtesy gone to waste
If you won't walk with me then just leave me and don't make it worse
Don't play off how easily I get attached—my love that tastes like a curse
Don't ever give me another smile then leave me all alone
Painfully I beg of you to stop and to end this tortuous song

Dance-Career-Ending Knee Injury and Surgery
August, 2006

Flo-Jo Rhyme

It's up to the King when it's finally done
They think they playin' with a game but it's God's own Son
I wish I had a flow like Jo could go
Sprintin' in the fast lane on the Olympics show—
But I—
plugged it in, my NiteLyte will glow
so if ya' didn't back then it's like "now ya' know"
It's so—so to tha sick to tha def
I learned it in the bass and in the treble clef
They used ta say "It's Li'l Miss Alicia Keys' "
But suddenly I found myself prayin' on my knees sayin',
"Lord save me please, I wanna live for you
Rep' Your name, rep' Your Word in everything I do"—
and it's true—
It's in my veins—I know He's got me gifted
But I'ma spit Him in my hooks so they don't get it twisted
I spit it for the thugz to tha girls wearin' Ugz
tha execs in the office and tha boys in tha club
I spit for the fatherless lookin' for a dad
and for the folks livin' life outside of dreams they had—
and it's sad—
we at a place where it's about our race, about our hair and what we wear —
the color of our face—
But it—
Ain't gonna change if I sit back stayin' silent
While gangs recruitin' babies—losin' kids ta violence
See time's runnin' out while record sales are gunnin'
When the essence of their hooks are turnin' drugs to funnin'
See they flirtin' with a lie and, to me, I think they know it
But I wonder what will happen on the day they choose ta show it

Random Rhyme

It's in my veins, it's how I always stay the same
It's in His name, and how He brought me outta' shame
It's in my fleau, and how I never let it go
And so ya' know, I'm comin' knockin' at ya' do'
I'm like a rock climber when I rock to tha top
And how I produce the Truth like a machine that won't stop
Just a smith skilled with a key and a lock
God's in control like a chef at a wok
I try to ta keep it aimed straight no matta' how they mock
I'm a souljah I told ya' I won't let it drop
Keepin' it colorful like artists in smocks
Wit' one eye on tha block and another on tha stock
Not the market but the Heavenly Bach
Wiped the slate clean with the bloodstained mop
So now the door's open and so is tha shop

Did You Know?

Did you know just what His interests were when He played outside?
Could you understand His destiny by looking in His eyes?
Many a day she watched Him, wondering what His future held.

Wednesday, December 13, 2006

Fearing Fearless

She's afraid to walk 'cause she thinks she'll fall
Afraid to run when she hears the call
Afraid because everyone just stands so tall
Afraid 'cause she's shorter, even when she gives her all
She's afraid of the venom in society's words
Afraid of the freedom in soaring like a bird
Afraid of beauty and afraid of her worth
Afraid of her name being dragged in the dirt
She's afraid of attention yet longing for love
Afraid of abandonment yet wanting a hug
Afraid of herself and afraid of man
Afraid of being fearless, when she knows that she can

Dreamin' Alone

I've got madness inside my head
Dreamin' up big dreams, aspirations while layin' in bed
Sometimes I wish it'd leave me alone
But then I guess it can't 'cause my destiny is written in stone
I'm on my own
It's like I'm runnin' this race by myself

Thursday, December 14, 2006 1:52 P.M.

Language Freak

If you know me I'm a language freak
I voice my gifts in everything I speak
That's why I don't know what I'm gonna be
So in the meantime I'm just a wannabe
So I speak in poetry, I speak in love
I speak in music from my Father above
I speak in writing and I speak in dance
I speak my life through this pen in my hand

Dead or Alive

I'm wanted dead or alive, but it's the latter
'cause Jesus is the One who makes my heart go "pitter-patter"

Friday, December 15, 2006

This Has Nothing to Do with You

I want to feel beautiful, but they keep pressing me down
And now my smile is nothing more than a frown turned upside-down
The only existent attraction is in the desire to cause me pain
And thus they trod all over me, with all their fortune and fame
Sometimes I truly wonder if it brings them any joy
To treat me like an object without feelings; like a toy
Do they see me as a robot, heartless with no pain?
Or is it off my hidden tears that they receive the power they gain?
But I cannot abandon my desire for beauty on the way they often treat me
Instead I have to hear God's voice and never let them defeat me

War

"Beautiful," where are you?
"Desirable," I cannot find you
In unison you hold the key that unlocks the destined
Does one of you end in pain?
Does one of you breed deception?
Are you a gift or are you a curse?
Beauty isn't always desirable, yet desirable is always beautiful
Beauty allures but for a trivial moment
Desirable encourages but someday will need this in return
One may have beauty and empty love, another desirability and abandonment
Beautiful and desirable, constantly at odds
But together . . .
You are powerful and meek, confident and sweet
Ready to be taken, ready to belong
Brave, secure, young, mature, wise, golden
You fear no one, you regret no averted eyes
For you know that it's coming, you don't worry
You have it together, both of you hand in hand
But whom should I choose, which should I want?
I admit I don't always believe; I don't want beauty if it would only impart fear
I don't want desirable if I'm not perceived as beautiful
You can't have it all, but what good is "all" when you're alone?
These were created to be enjoyed, not hoarded, not feared, not cried over
But they can only call her beautiful for so long before she'll wonder where the *enjoyer* is

The Gift

I don't know if you exist
But I know that it would be bliss
To give to you this special gift
The gift that is my very first kiss.

I-N-V-I-S-I-B-L-E, for the God with X-ray Vision

It's a fact—we want to be seen, heard and recognized. From birth, we've gradually squeezed ourselves into a mold of an inherent desire to not only be important, revered, respected and appreciated, but ultimately esteemed—praised and glorified. This is something we are taught from our surroundings, but also something we simply crave. Because love and care for one another is not a thing to be taught, our initial instinct is to look out for ourselves. If glory is not directed toward us, but for someone else's works, then it is considered worthless to us. Likewise, if someone else is to be recognized and applauded, we immediately (though we wouldn't always admit it) feel a sudden need for attention. This is from the humblest person to the proudest. But doesn't it make sense to want a "pat on the back" for something you've done? Aren't you worth it? Or is it just the defective society we live in and the superficial media that engraves this so-called "truth" into our morals? Though we shouldn't have to, we ask ourselves why we should step aside for someone else to receive glory. Why let someone else steal your spotlight? We need instant gratification—to us, there is no such thing as a deed done in secret that can be rewarded. To us, this is true even when the deed was not only done by us, but when somebody else ends up taking the credit for it. Wipe that frown off your face, because you've thought, felt, and reacted to these things yourself, though you may not admit it—we all have.

We all have a yearning to be first and foremost, because we've learned, unfortunately, to confuse attention and praise for love. And though love can be displayed through acknowledging, appreciating and respecting another's works, it is not confined to those actions alone. Our oftentimes twisted desire to be appreciated will always be with us, since we are dealing with this thing called "flesh". But what we are forgetting is that God not only respects the invisible, but he sees it. God is not limited to the provincial eyes of man, and his vision is 20/20 to the infinite power. Thus, shouldn't our actions respond to that? Shouldn't we trust God's character and believe that He is watching us? Or are we really so desperate that we can only feel the temporary touch of man's reward, but not the eternal blessing of God's favor?

Whether we learn to be invisible to man and visible to God in this life or not, He is still watching, and unfortunately, since we are oftentimes so concerned and obsessed with pleasing man, displaying our works and begging for applause, His eyes are witnessing our visible sin of trampling our brothers and sisters more often than our invisible, sincere deeds. The true intentions of our hearts would be revealed if God were to suddenly cease rewarding our deeds in secret. Who would still do them . . . would you? Would I? Would you still serve your brother even when there isn't any reward in sight? Pretend that God didn't promise to reward you in this life or the next as you go throughout your week, and see what you learn about the true colors of your heart.

"Be careful not to do your 'acts of righteousness' before men, to be seen by them. If you do, you will have no reward from your Father in heaven. So when you give to the needy, do not announce it with trumpets, as the hypocrites do in the synagogues and on the streets, to be honored by men. I tell you the truth, they have received their reward in full. But when you give to the needy, do not let you left hand know what your right hand is doing, so that your giving may be in secret. Then your Father, who sees what is done in secret, will reward you." Matthew 6:1-4.

Black History Series

A New Song

Our voices rise to heaven
Our prayers in the kettle
Religion's supposed to be our savior
But our souls is never settled
So we sings 'bout things we just don't have,
Things we sho' can't see
We sings with all our power and might and give God every plea
We sings at day, we sings the whole day long
But now, we sings for the Savior to teach us a new song

Black History Series

My Side

Glistening waters, salt dries our lips
Root of all evil, sting of the whip
Money's their freedom,
Labor our chains
But our eyes are on heaven, to help us stay sane
My mother was beaten, my father has died
Packed on a ship, and stripped of our pride
And now comes the shore, the "land of the free"
My skin is the reason this freedom isn't for me

Black History Series

Victory

Emancipation Proclamation, it reached our ears with gladness
We stayed up watching and praying to put an end to our sadness
But yet we sang of victory even when our hands were bound
And Momma once said that even man couldn't keep our hopes down
For someone else had conquered, someone above a president
Someone who could feel as man yet make a heart His residence
So it's victory over the labor, victory over the sorrow
Victory over our scar and victory over tomorrow
Victory for all who believe, not victory by human hands
But victory over the past, and that because of the God-Man

Does Jesus Walk?

Does Jesus walk? Or is it that just the hook to a song? And it means nothing if you don't
see what's going on.
Yes, Jesus walks, but He means what he says when He talks
But it seems like today we want a silent Jesus—the One Who only saves
and Who will never leave us
We want a Jesus who's all about the actions, and we just don't want the
reciprocal to the fraction
You just want a Jesus who'll get you outta' your mess, a situation He
didn't bless
So you forget it's a test
But God doesn't talk just to hear His own voice
He gives you good advice so you'll make the right choice
God saw the end before you saw the beginning
And He sure didn't die just so you could keep on sinning.

Finally Got My Copyright

Finally got my copyright certificate in the mail today! Along with a scam letter from some record company trying to "re-record" my music and pay me royalties . . . Thank God for online research. . Finished a story I started when I had my surgery . . . It was written from experience, so yeah . . . Maybe I'll edit it enough to work up the courage to submit it to some publisher. . . I'm feeling like I'm making some kind of progress, finally, though the world will probably never know about any of this.

This is why I'll be a starving speech-language pathologist and die happy! Hobbies are hobbies. I'll learn that someday. . I'm definitely starting to see the results of not being able to do cardio—I'm feeling them, too. I feel like I'm underwater and sluggish…I hate it. I'm used to feeling pumped and energetic. I need to somehow get back to cardio exercises where air fills my lungs. In the past year, I had gotten into working out regularly and really enjoyed it, but now I'm feeling like I'm missing something. With my knee messed up, I don't know what to do. And it's crazy to feel like you're being pulled underwater but can't do anything to get yourself back up to the surface—my hands are tied, and it's all resting on my knee…so many things are resting on my knee. Ugh. I'm trying not to get frustrated, but it's not always easy. I'll ask my doc about it when I go see him, I guess. Maybe he'll know what to do. This was supposed to be about progress. Lol. Oh well. There are two sides to every story.

High School Graduation Speech

Middle Tennessee Home Education Association Graduation Ceremony
Two Rivers Baptist Church, Nashville, Tennessee

Fellow graduates of the Class of 2007, parents, other family members and friends:
I would like to thank the MTHEA Graduation Committee for the great honor of speaking on this memorable occasion.

On behalf of my fellow classmates I would also like to thank every parent who has had to re-learn Algebra, Chemistry, fractions, "Please Excuse My Dear Aunt Sally," SQ3R, and all of that other once-easy but suddenly-challenging subject matter. It is because of your diligence and care that we are here today.

Imagine you're at the mall, you've had a long day of shopping, you're tired and ready to go home, your bags are so loaded that your fingers are throbbing, and your feet are in desperate need of elevation. But just as you're about to head for the exit, having just grabbed a sugar-coated pretzel from the stand, out of the corner of your eye you see someone coming, holding a piece of paper in one hand, a friendly smile on their face, a pen extended. You try to quicken your pace but they're too fast and step in front of you.

"What do you expect from yourself?" they ask, handing you the paper.

You look down.

A simple survey, entitled "Are You Afraid to Touch the Sky?" On it there are three boxes from which to choose. You smirk, but your amused smile quickly vanishes as you study the paper:

"Everything
Something
Nothing"

the boxes read.

"What do I expect from myself?" you ask.

Which would you check? If I had a clock to time you with, how long would it take you to check a box? Would your pretzel be abandoned, your bags dropped and feet forgotten? Or would you quickly jot anything down without a second thought? . . .What do you expect from yourself? Everything, something, or nothing? Are you afraid to touch the sky?

I've always been afraid of heights. I was the kid on the playground who had to take a few deep breaths and mumble fervent prayers before downing the good old metal firehouse pole. And I remember laying in the grass in my backyard, looking up at the expansive sky and thinking, "God, why is it that I can't fall into the sky if it's right below me?" After all,

97

the sky does seem to hover beneath you when it's all you can see—it seems so far yet so close you could touch it.

My mom answered that question soon enough, and the answer was, of course, "gravity" —that thing that astronauts defy, birds chuckle at, and John Mayer could buy a Cadillac off of. [sic]

Gravity has been fought for centuries through attempts to construct planes and wings. To jets and rockets. We conquer this powerful force because of the mere aspect of curiosity . . . and perhaps a calling to overcome the seemingly impossible.

But in order to even *dare* to achieve such feats, man must have once *expected* himself to be able to do so in the first place. After all, God make work what it is for a reason—a challenge to overcome, in order that God may show us what He can do through us. But after we dare to *dream*, we have to then dare to expect.

Dreaming is more than what you do when you sleep. It's also been pinned with the definition of a sort of appealing goal which causes us to smile and hope—making our hearts skip when it crosses our minds at work or during homework. But as pertinent as dreams are, we often fail to see that they are only the *beginning, the mere seed of something greater.* Benjamin Franklin must have dreamed at one point and time; *something* must have caused him to wonder what would happen if he flew a kite in a storm because you and I both know that it wouldn't have been *us* out there doing something that dangerous. After all, we *already* know electricity exists, right?

Christopher Columbus also dreamed of a round earth, and set sail on a perilous journey to prove it. But would you do this to prove that point? Hopefully not, because you've seen photos of the earth from outer space!

And what about building a plane like the Wright brothers? Would you do it to show all the world that man can take flight? . . . Hmm, probably not. A good number of you may have flown out here by plane this weekend!

So I have to ask: what is it about certain dreams that makes them fact? Isn't it interesting to note that many dreams and aspirations are of things that will come to pass or already exist? Why is that? . . .

"What do you expect from yourself? Everything, something, or nothing?"

Are you afraid to touch the sky?

Time is ticking by quickly now, and you're starting to sweat over your survey. You don't have an answer—that is, not an honest one. How can you choose "everything" when you know you're not planning on applying for that job or studying for that test—starting that eating-right plan or opening that dusty Bible . . . .

What do you expect from yourself? Everything, something, or nothing? Are you afraid to touch the sky? . . .

When you drove here this morning, you moved along roads—paved and finished— streets which construction workers have already completed for you. You didn't worry about the church existing on an island, because you expected it to be reachable—attainable . . . And yet, I wonder if you could say that about your life—the path to *your* dreams. Have you ever tried to picture it as though it were a single road on a plane, extending into the horizon? You probably couldn't see the end clearly, but you knew it was there. After all, every dreamer, whether their dream shifted over time or remained the same, has ended up *somewhere*.

But what happens if you *don't* dream? —if you shy away from *expecting something, hoping for something, anticipating something?*

What do you expect from yourself? Everything, something, or nothing? Are you afraid to touch the sky? . . .

Have you ever heard that God can only steer a moving car? You see, that applies to dreaming. We may have dreams, but if we never take action to pursue them, or get our "cars" moving, then what is there for God to steer? Maybe we should examine why people are afraid to dream because, get this, the mere fear of success! Oddly enough, as good and wonderful as success is, it's also intimidating. And for this reason, a lot of people don't even want to think about it, but would rather that it fall into their laps in a few years or so. Being sold-out for Christ is an example of this type of intimidation—probably landing at number one on the top ten list of "Things that Intimidate Teenagers."

Besides, if you plan on living until you're 100, you might as well put off the challenging or "uncomfortable" things until later, right?

What do you expect from yourself? Everything, something or nothing? Are you afraid to touch the sky?

Now having spent a good five minutes considering these questions, you take a seat on a nearby mall bench, the words on the survey paper jumping out at you. But suddenly, there's something written at the bottom in fine print; something you must have missed before. It reads:

"There *is* no right or wrong answer"

— It's a survey, for goodness' sake! But if there *could* be a *right* answer, it would not be to expect everything, not even something, and certainly not "nothing" of yourself. But rather, it would be to expect "anything" from the One who created you to walk the path He's *already* paved for you. After all, *He's the One who drew the map!*

You set the paper down. You stop. You think. You put the neglected pretzel on hold. .

What *do* you expect from yourself? Greatness? Failure? An okay ending? A happy ending?

Maybe it's time for you to expect anything that's good; any dream given you by God.

As the Marianne Williamson quote goes:

"Our deepest fear is not that we are inadequate. Our deepest fear is that we are powerful beyond measure. It is our *light*, not our darkness, that most frightens us. We ask ourselves, Who am I to be brilliant, gorgeous, talented, fabulous? Actually, who are you *not* to be? You are a child of God. Your playing small does not serve the world. . . We are all meant to shine, as children do. We were born to make manifest the glory of God that is within us. . . And as we let our own light shine, we unconsciously give other people permission to do the same. . ." (Williamson 190-191).

And with God's translation:

"For we are God's workmanship, created in Christ Jesus to do good works, which God prepared in advance for us to do." Ephesians 2:10

What do you expect from yourself? Anything, everything, something or nothing? Are you afraid to touch the sky?

One day, a man walked into a cartographer's shop, looking to have a map created. Inside the shop were beautiful maps hanging on the walls. Some of the maps were big, others small—some had many streets and intersections, and others were simple. As the man waited for the cartographer to appear from the back room, he studied the maps carefully, and soon noted that each one had its own "x" marking a particular spot. Puzzled by this, the man wondered why the marks were there. After all, this wasn't a treasure-map shop, was it?

Before the man could consider any further, a voice sounded from the back room. The cartographer appeared.

"What can I help you with?" He asked.

The man stroked his chin, then replied, "I would like to have a map made, but first I'd like to know your credentials and exactly *why* you have "x" s marked on each map. Is this some kind of treasure-map shop?"

But the cartographer only smiled.

"You *could* say that this is a treasure-map shop, since each map leads to treasures. And as for my credentials—take a look at each map. This one, for example, was made for a client who was a songwriter. He was the youngest of many brothers, and when he followed my map, it led him to victory over a giant, a job as the government's top musician, and later his own ascension to the presidency.

"And take this map, for example—I made it for a girl who came to me, an orphan, living in a country that was not her native land. I mapped a path for her which led to winning the title of 'Miss Persia,' marriage to a mighty president, and eventually saving her people from a would-be terrorist attack.

"If you're still in doubt of my credentials, let me show you this map—the one I made for an atypical young man—an outsider. He wasn't at all popular, wore clothes considered to be 'funny,' and ate strange things. I drew a map that would usher him to proclaiming the coming of the world's greatest hero.

"But that's not all—I made a map for a riches-to-rags man with a stutter, leading him to admiration and the role of guiding a large nation out of captivity. And of course, there's the young woman who was poverty-stricken after her husband died. When she followed the map I gave her, she married a rich man and started a family.

"You see, you are right in assuming that my maps are treasure maps, because they each hold an "x" marking the spot. But it's still always up to the person following the map as to whether or not they find the treasure. My maps are easy to follow, and all you have to do is stay on the right path in order to reach the treasure."

The cartographer finished, and the man quickly requested a map of his own. But when he expected the cartographer to ask him to come back in a week or so for the finished product, the cartographer only smiled and brought out the map, already finished and "marked," from his desk drawer. It had already been created—even before the man entered the shop.

God is the ultimate Cartographer of every life—yours and mine. He marks each map with an "x'" indicating the treasure awaiting us. Your treasure may be a career as a doctor, a lawyer, a singer, an actor—it may be an answered prayer, a scholarship, a job, an idea, a business. God knows your personal "x," and if you follow the path carefully, you find your marked treasure.

So what do you expect from yourself? Better yet, what do you expect from your **Cartographer**? Do you expect anything from Him? Everything, something, or just nothing? Do you question his credentials, as did the man in the shop?

For those of you who are afraid to touch the sky, consider this: If God paved it, you *can* walk it. And as you graduate and move into another season of your life, don't expect everything from yourself, since everything can weigh you down and burn you out; and don't just expect *something* either, since you're a child of the Maker of all—and certainly don't expect "nothing," since you're loved by a caring God. But rather expect anything, and don't settle for the sky being the limit. Because when it all comes down to it, the only one who has the true say-so on your future is the Ultimate Cartographer with the pen and creativity which puts even Tolkien to shame—not peers, not generational trends, not even *your own fear*, if you let it, can erase what God has *already* mapped.

So what do you expect from yourself? Are you afraid to touch the sky? Fellow students, graduating Class of 2007, I say we shoot for the *stars*, and touch the sky on the *way*.

Application Essay for High School Graduation Speech

I would like to address my peers because I believe that my generation is quick to believe the lie that our success is either non-existent, confined to the standards placed on our shoulders or dependent upon the measure of someone else's degree of success—a peer, parent or generation. For this reason, it would be an honor to remind my peers that our success is like a stretch of finished road that must only be traveled, since we have been given the gift of potential from our Father, to be more than our pasts, failures and even our oftentimes-timid standards. We should shoot for the stars and kiss the sky on the way.

War II

Last year I wrote a poem called "War" and in between the rhymes I asked
what beauty's really for
This year I've learned a lot and true, I've learned to love myself whether you do or not—
But my—young heart questions—and—
keeps on guessin'—what—
All their eyes see—though— they can't see me— see?—
I got a wall up to keep my heart protected
Just in case somebody comes along with love defective
Now, calm down fellas
That don't mean you should be jealous of my primary love—and that's
The Man above
'Cause when a girl guards her heart, they say that something must be wrong
But let a fella play it safe—they'll say he's got it goin' on!
But anyway, I won't dwell on that subject any longer
Besides, your opposition's only gonna make me stronger
So back to the question of beauty's worth
See I think it's other people that's gon' always leave us hurt
-'Cause-
She has *this* skin tone that he wants
-or- She's got *that* kind of figure to flaunt
Ha, you know it's funny how it comes down to tha honey
with tha real smooth talk and tha real loose walk
But if a wise gal comes along most fellas run the otha' way
Because they knew off tha bat they wouldn't get it today
-But hey-
let's not forget that even "nice" guys play the game
They can act like they love you, but you're really the same
-as-
All the otha' cute little girls that they knew and used
So every nice guy ain't gon' always be true
So I got a set of questions to throw up for debate
And by the end of this rhyme maybe truth will demonstrate
Number 1: Why do church boys always want a perfect girl
-like-
Every girl's Beyoncé and a gift to the world
True, I know that Eve was pleasing Adam's eye—and that's a fact

103

But perfect women don't exist—go find a needle in a haystack
Number 2: Why does skin tone often tend to lead a man's decision?
I thought God created different tones and hues with such precision
It saddens me that black girls wanna hate each other's tints
When in reality we on the same side of the fence!
(*Cough, cough*)
Number 3: the one that gets to me is how fellas judge a girl only based on what they see
They forget that Size 2 don't mean she's gonna be true
-or that-
Innocent face means what you say—she's gonna do
(Oh, oh!)
Number fo', the last one to go—tha one ta show—how fellas really run the show
Hey ladies:
Why you always chasin' after men
-when-
Back in the day, *they* were the ones to fight to win
Not you, so confused, end up alone in the end
-and you-
Hate ya' sister
-over-
A random mister
I'll bet you 20 dolla's he's just only gonna diss her
(*Conclude*)
I guess it's true about it bein' a man's world
-to an extent-
Though,'cause Jesus cares for every broken girl (*and* boy)
It's only Satan try'na steal, kill and destroy
And we fall for that lie every time we lose sight
Try'na hate on each other when we down in a fight
So beauty, do you only mean a fairy princess?
Bound to get love but by droppin' your defenses?
No. There's inner beauty too, the one that's gonna last
The one that grabs a man's heart—the one that holds it fast
-So-
We can write another book, We can sing another song,
We can host another conference 'til we learn what's *really* wrong
See the problem ain't a lack of *women* who will take this stand
'Cause true beauty's *truly* understood when taught by a Man.

I Can't Complain

I can't complain
Because I live in a house with heat and air conditioning
I can't complain
Because I am surrounded by people who love me
I can't complain
Because I have food to eat and clean water to drink
I can't complain
Because I graduated from high school and now attend college
I can't complain
Because I have a keyboard and the ability to make music
I can't complain
Because I have incredible friends
I can't complain
Because I can see and hear and feel
I can't complain
Because my heart has been beating for all of these years
I can't complain
Because though I can't physically dance like I used to, I can dance in my dreams
I can't complain
Because all of the hobbies I love, no one can take my love for them away from me
I can't complain
Because I can help others and give my time and talent to other people
I can't complain
Because I don't have to go to a priest to talk to my Heavenly Father
I can't complain
Because I can walk into my neighborhood street right this second and shout "Jesus"
without fear of being shot
I can't complain
Because I don't need to watch a movie or listen to a hit song to be entertained
I can't complain
Because God reminds me that He loves me every time I look at the stars
I can't complain
Because I get to see Jesus face-to-face someday . . . and nothing can compare to that.

It's NiteLyte and when I throw it down I fight like I'm sparrin' and it's the last round
'Cause the clock's on and the countdown is gettin' lower
I gotta spit tha truth because this light I gotta show—uh
Most rappers won't say what they need to say but
I'm a speak tha truth and show a different Way Yo,
What is in the heart is what is gonna flow out
So let me preach tha Gospel so that Jesus Christ can show out
-VERSE-
Lemme put it like this in a way you'll understand
It's a song about a Hero, a Savior, a man
-But-
Think about that person who put your safety first
The One didn't mind their name draggin' in the dirt
Yo, think about that love one you always took for granted
Think about the best friend with whom you could be candid
Clean cut, nice smile, walkin' wit' a smooth swagga'
But it was all about attention, nothin' else mattered
You said you feelin' me and tried ta make it not seem
That you were waitin' on them digits—I was too keen
Talks on the phone, every otha' weekend
With every compliment my heart began to weaken
Some tried to tell me love was not what you were seekin'
I didn't listen 'till some details started leakin'
They say you had a job, career of spittin' mad game
Not just with rappin' but with knowin' every girl's name
I didn't wanna think that you had prior practice
But I had to face the truth and realize the fact is
I don't wanna be a number on a long list
I don't wanna be tha 52nd girl you kissed
I'm a child of Christ, waitin' for the weddin'
You got something else in mind, then you can gladly get ta steppin'
BRIDGE/VERSE 3
Hubby has gotta be, what ya' gonna be 4 me
Leadin' tha family and reppin' Jesus with me
It's gotta be 4 real and not just in the way we feel
We gotta be friends even when it all ends
We gotta fall in love and in our callin'
We gotta hold each otha' up when 1 is fallin'

The counterfeits treat love like it's worthless
But marriage is the bond that loves with purpose

Romantic Games

Romantic games we played
More like a masquerade
Was a disguise we made
And love I always forbade
I didn't wanna be anything more than friends
But you, bein' a guy,
The chase, it never ends

Love with Purpose

A poetic plea for you and me
so we can get to see how it can be
-if we-
Be the ones to separate from the crowd
Step into the Son
And let our light shine loud
-'cause-
I believe that we can love
With purpose
-and-
I believe that
We can swim
To the surface
Take a breath
Of love's freshest air
Christ is the Truth that we must share

Learning to Love

I'm learning to love even when my heart is crushed
I'm learning to love when they betray my trust
I'm learning to love even when they see right through me
I'm learning to love even when they try to use me
I'm learning to love when they act like they're above me
I'm learning to love when they themselves don't wanna love me
I'm learning to love 'cause that's God's greatest command
I'm learning to love because with Christ I know I can

Tuesday, February 19, 2008

Another Song Finished

It felt so good to feel keys beneath my fingers again!

Finished another full-length song with a sturdy hook, 2 verses and a bridge. This is BIG for someone who sticks mainly to instrumentals. Since I don't have equipment that records vocals, I will just probably just post the instrumental track after I snag a copyright and what not. I really feel like I'm finding myself lyrically, though. My style is quick, tightly-packed and comfortable, just as I like it for myself. I feel I'm getting better at telling stories and expressing myself through rhyme. I don't freestyle, but my rhyming abilities feel more natural now—as though I could rhyme on any topic and take just a few minutes to write it up. Now if I could just find somebody to spit and sing on the track for me . . .

Naked

They all want something from me
Entertaining their perceptions of me
In private they measure me
Their love is empty
It's about what they can take from me
Thus their love is lust
There is no respect
I'm the vessel to their success
I'm the jewelry around their neck
Tricked into giving my devotion and friendship
I'd take a bullet for them; they might stand and watch me die,
Thinking, "There goes my success."
Second-guessed
Ridiculed
Naked
Stripped by their eyes
Inhumane, cruel and selfish
They watch me as I lie
The ground is cold like their hearts for me
I wish I could hide, so that they can't see me
So hurt I can barely rhyme
My gift is swallowed
Instead I write until all the blood drains
My heart is stabbed
Punctured by deception
I wish I hadn't trusted
I wish that I had questioned
I can feel for them but they only pretend to feel for me
In order to steal my trust, my heart, to save it for a rainy day
They bring up the past, use it as bait
"Remember when?" they question me so that they can have their way
I only want to be cared about
I don't even need it in deed
Just promise me you feel for me and off my friendship you will not feed
Love is sacrificial
It's not all about you.

I'll Speak the Truth

I'll speak the Truth
'Cause to my friends I'm relayin'
How he saved my soul, eternal debts been paid-in
How can I keep my young ways pure?
It's all about obedience and that's how I'll endure

Spring, 2008

Dear Someone

Dear someone
I think about you so much these days
I think about the time when I'll have you for always
In all ways, I try to keep my heart for you pure
I try to keep my love guarded, tryin' to endure
I pray I never mistake someone else for you
I pray I don't forget to keep on prayin' for you
'Cause I know it's not easy for you in this world
And I know that on the way to me, you'll meet many girls
I just hope that none of them break your heart
But if they do, know that I can be your new start

Standin' Back and Lookin'

Standin' back and lookin' at my circumstances
And all the times I ran away from open chances
Reminiscing on my life and all the choices I made
And all the hopeful dreams that I decided to save

Diagnosed with Malignant
Brain Tumor
June, 2008

The Wall

I stand before a wall
Bathed in its shadow, it makes me feel so small
The angle is 90, my accomplishments are behind me
Day and night I pray and hope that help will soon find me
Here, it's dark, yet still I'm unafraid
My eyes can distinguish the rocky surface without any aid
Somehow it assures me that I won't stay in the shadow much longer
Voices from my left and right, I can see I'm not alone
They warn me that I won't make it if I do it on my own
In yearning awe I watch them scale the wall
The sun peaks around its corners; they aren't afraid they might fall
Amazed, I watch their feet stick to the rock like glue
Crying out, I plead with God that I can scale it too
Horizontal to the ground, in faith they move higher
So fearlessly they climb, and I know I crave their fire
Now they've reached the top, they thank the Lord on their knees
My heart becomes warm when they look down and hold their hands out to me
I'm afraid that I won't make it, afraid to take the first step;
Afraid that halfway or a quarter up is as far as I can get
But suddenly my fear is silenced, forced to submit to the Voice
The darkness is forced to flee, because with God, there's no other choice
"With Me, you can walk up this mountain,
With Me you will always be safe
With Me, all things are possible, if you would only have the faith
This is not based on the wall that you see
No, faith is a reflection of your hope and trust in Me."

The Moment

Yo, I'm standin' up against the wall and feelin' only two feet tall
'Cause to the world I gave it all
But I can finally hear Your call
And I ain't gonna run away 'cause I can see the sunny day
'Cause for my soul, Your life You gave
And now it's time to be your slave
I'm turnin' from my wicked ways
I'm dyin' just to see Your face
And since my past has been erased
Now I can start to run the race
And I ain't gonna look back when I take off
But like a thief I'm gonna risk it all like Bernie Madoff
You made all things new in my life, so I'm finally gonna walk in the Truth
And I'll sacrifice by puttin' up the sight and steppin' from the darkness right into the
Father's light
'Cause we live in the last days
Ain't no time to hesitate
Either real or am I fake?
Now I got a choice to make
Tired of all the heartache
Ready for something safe
Ready 'cause I just can't wait
Ready 'cause I'm 'bout to break

Chorus

This is the moment
This is the moment
This is the moment
(that I give my life to You)
'Cause I'm lookin' for, I'm lookin' for
I'm lookin' for just something true

(repeat)

I'm lookin' for
I'm lookin' for
Someone like You

The Only One to Save Me

The only One to save me
You're the One who made me
Fearfully and wonderfully
Now my blinded eyes can see
How Your love has set me free
And how Your love has captured me
Sinful ways I'm gonna flee
All the shame is leavin' me
Walkin' upright now
Given new sight now
How can I keep my young ways pure?
By obeyin' Your Word for sure
How can I keep this to myself?
No to my friends I gotta tell
With everyone I've gotta share
That there is someone who cares
Just like me, you can be new
Jesus' blood is for you, too
He's knockin', won't you let Him in?
Let Him set you free from sin

May 2, 2009

I Have a Secret

Current mood: : | pensive

I haven't blogged in a while, mainly because I really didn't have anything to say. This spring has been busy for me. Lots of traveling, pretty much. Without being in school or working, I've had plenty of free time during the week, and since I'm feeling completely back to my old self from recovering from treatment, I feel like I'm racing through slow-motion. By "racing," I mean that life is moving very fast, even though I'm not really doing anything "significant," in the world's standard, that is. Meaning, I'm not in school working toward that degree my extended family would hope I have. Not really doing what most 20-year-olds do. A lot of people ask me what I "do," meaning, "Do I have a life?" And I answer honestly, explaining briefly that I work on my writing (fiction novels) and my music (songwriting). And the interesting thing is, my writing, my creative communication gift, is really the part of me that used to be buried deep beneath my brainy, Phi Theta Kappa, daughter-of-a-doctor side. Pretty much no one knew about my songwriting hopes and dreams when I was slaving under a full college course-load. Nobody knew that I'd written two novels and was on the brink of sending one off to publishers. But I'm not all that sure that I even have a chance with an audience, sometimes. If I even *have* an audience. It's like knowing some big, exciting news flash that I can't share. It can drive you crazy.

And yet, now that my college, average 20-year-old's lifestyle has been put on hold because of last summer's diagnosis, I've been able to fully embrace my creative gifting.

But it still feels like a big secret, and I'm not sure how I feel about that.

If I had one wish for my creative passions, if someone were to say that they could grant me one dream come true regarding them, my answer would be to make them public. Now, I've asked myself lately if that's a selfish desire. If it's wrong for me to want to share the things I've written with the world, because I doubt if it's good enough, if anyone will understand it and see it the way I do. I worry because *everyone else* is satisfied with getting through college and getting married and having kids. I would be too, don't get me wrong, but it's so strange sometimes to have such a raging passion for writing and music and being unsuccessful in sharing it. I guess it's really my fault that I'm stuck like this. The only person stopping me is myself.

But my answer to my question of whether or not I'm being selfish is no. When I write a story, yes, I do it for the joy it brings me, and to please the Lord, to give that gift right back to Him. And I would be just fine if I was playing my music and reading my stories for only His ears alone. But I also write with people in mind. I write things based on dreams I have, on ideas, on things from the outside world. I write to encourage and inspire others.

I just haven't really released everything I've made to those "others" yet, and I wonder what's taking me so long, what with all of this time on my hands.

So until I make my move, it's still my little secret.

As for college . . . yeah, it would still be sweet to keep going. The only thing that stopped me was my illness; it's not like I just gave up. And I still have that other side of me, my passion for language, for therapy. And when I go in for my next standard MRI at Duke, a week before my birthday (fun, huh?) I'll pass that same Speech-Language/Audiology clinic once again, and I know I'll feel that familiar longing, as I always do . . .

10:54 A.M.
May 13, 2009

Another clean MRI
10:10 A.M.
.

Jul 14, 2009

Gotta Keep Faith
UPDATE:

I had originally posted this Monday after getting those results back, and was on the road and typing on my cell phone, so I wasn't able to go into much detail, but I wanted to inform everyone who has so kindly been praying for me and encouraging me through this trial for this difficult year.

Yesterday the doctor showed me the MRI, where you can see the empty crater still where the tumor used to be. Only now it also shows a small, blurry area just outside of that crater, which he does not believe to be tumor because he said they usually don't look that way. But he said that the radiologist who first reviewed the scan thinks I should come back sooner to be safe and make sure. So as opposed to coming back in 2 months as was the original plan, they want me back in 1 month. /4 weeks. So I'll be back at Duke getting the next MRI in August

I won't front. The news took a while to register, and you have a lot of time alone with your thoughts when you're traveling. I'm kind of up and down emotionally, and had some moments where it did sink in and I zoned out and felt the numbness kicking in, so I would really appreciate that you pray for my emotions and that they don't get the best of me leading into this next MRI, that I can focus as I get the final preps in for starting the Fall semester and that I'm walking by faith and joyful.

This battle can feel very stressful, I will admit. It's hard to have joy and normalcy in life when you have to pack up and leave home every few weeks to get a stressful scan done. My stomach always gets filled with butterflies and I'm just on edge. It's difficult to not allow that nervousness to seep into my everyday life. I had an MRI just a few days before my birthday, which made me not look forward to my birthday in May this year. .

And also, if you could, please pray for my family. The biggest struggle in this for me is them. Often I've felt like I've changed everything for us, and that I'm a burden because of what happened to me. Not that it's my fault that I got diagnosed with cancer last year, but . . . well, it's hard to be the reason why things are different for us, and I don't want them to share in my worrying. I can handle being anxious alone. That's just how it is and I have to deal with my emotions as I'm a "big girl" now. But I hate to see them feeling the same way and I just wish that none of this would harm them.

All in all, I have a risen Savior who can help me carry the load. I just need to keep learning to not let my emotions get the best of me. There's a Name greater than this trial.

Original Blog Post from Monday on my cell:

So they found a small blurry spot on the MRI. My doctor doesn't think it looks like tumor, but wants me back in 4 weeks just to be safe. Could you please pray? I get nervous and depressed at times so this is a bit hard. Prayerfully, I won't be freaking out with worry for the next few weeks. I'm also getting ready 4 college so this can add 2 the stress. Kinda' feel like I've been carrying a weight around 4 a year, and this summer hasn't been easy. . . . God is faithful. I just need to take a breather and let go of this weight and let Jesus fight my battle for me.

2:19 P.M.
Jul 29, 2009

The Thorn of a Rose

Painted in poetry so that no one will know
Of the pain deep inside that just cannot be shown
For to know is to feel, to feel is to hurt
And no one else but the poet deserves to be dragged through this dirt
What is it like to be the thorn of a rose?
What guilt must it feel when, to friends, it is a foe?
All that it desires is to grow and to love
But its prick leaves a wound when others near for a hug
Though it means no harm, someone always pays
Thus the thorn would rather push the ones it loves away
To spare them the worrying, anxiety and tears
Because living as a burden to others is the thorn's greatest fear

- "The Thorn of a Rose" by NiteLyte

2:11 A.M.
Aug 16, 2009   I Can't Write Well Anymore, But . . .

I'm trying to get up and not down
Tryin' to have faith and not frown
All through my life I have found
That Christ is the only love around
Even when I'm in fear I might drown
He rescues me to solid ground
In all of my ideas I can see
This dreamer that sleeps inside of me
And maybe someday she'll be free
And not prone to doubt so easily 'Cause I got madness inside of my head
Dreamin' up big dreams, aspirations, while layin' in bed
Sometimes I wish it'd leave me alone

But then again, I guess it can't, 'cause my destiny is written in stone
I freestyle in my style every once in a while
But especially in trials
'Cause then my brain, it goes wild Like the flowin' of the Nile
It just goes on for miles and miles
'Till I reach for the dial and I switch up the station
Time to crank the volume up, no more hesitation
Even though it's difficult, all the pain that I've been facin'
Best believe my walk with Christ will keep on steady pacin'
A sensation, like fire shut up in my bones
Let me—let me rhyme the truth
Holy Spirit read my groans
Send 'em to Him on the throne
So I'll no longer feel alone
Like a diamond, precious stone
You got me in the process
Straighten what's crooked, like I got a process
Let me runaway no more
Let me open up the door
Let me welcome You inside
So I can walk in what's in store
But truth is, You never left me
Though I second guessed Thee
Now I'd lose a hand for You, makin' me a lefty
I know You gotta test me
Gotta see what's left in me
Gotta work on Stephanie
Help me so that I can see

- by NiteLyte

10:37 P.M.
Aug 19, 2009

Still in Battle
Getting a chemo infusion just hours after learning that there's new tumor was tough—kind of unreal. .

I don't know what the new chemo pill will be like, but the side-effects are about the same as the last one (decreased appetite, hair-thinning, low blood counts). I start taking the oral chemo tonight, so we'll see. . . . It's so strange, though, to know that something dangerous is in your head when you don't even have any side-effects. This feels a bit like a replay of last year, only without the pain. It's unreal, but I'll get through it with the Lord's help.

Please pray for my family. I don't want them to worry. It hurts me when they worry.
12:03 P.M.

Sep 6, 2009

My Dream Come True

No one knew what I was talking about when I told them what I wanted to do in and after college. Maybe a few, but not many. Even after I explained it, it was still a little "out there" to them. And that's okay.

But last week, when I walked through the doors of my school . . . it was like being the little "Ugly Duckling" finally come home to her family. (I'm being melodramatic.) .)

Let me explain:

I want to be a speech-language pathologist. I've known this for years. What is a speech-language pathologist, you're almost undeniably asking yourself? They are therapists who specialize in helping people with speech disorders ranging from lisps, stuttering, speech problems resulting from mental illness or traumatic brain injury, pitch problems, swallowing problems, fluency, articulation, and many more to list. They help people of all ages, but many help children, which I think is what I want to do.

I only knew basic information about this profession until last week (and obviously I'm still learning!). But it was so amazing to get to meet my teachers, who are SLPs (speech-language pathologists) and work in a speech clinic that serves the community on campus. It was also especially fulfilling for me because of my history with the school I've transferred to.

You see, although I knew I wanted to be an SLP when I graduated high school, I didn't go straight to the school I am now which offers the classes and degree in that field. I did community college instead because I wasn't sure if I could take the speech classes without first doing general ed courses. So I opted to save money and start in community college, then transfer to the university.

Fast forward to the end of my second semester/first year in community college. Everything was looking great, I was ready to go to the next step, my grades were excellent (praise the Lord), but then the first bomb dropped. The university, the place I'd dreamed about, cried about, prayed about, wanted to meet the teachers at and someday work for, said no. They rejected my high school transcript because it was a homeschool document· So there was lots of communication, travelling to the campus, phone calls, miscommunication, drama, tears. I felt like I'd gotten my 4.0 GPA for nothing and the door to my passion had shut. I felt like they didn't believe that I'd actually earned that GPA - that I was a fraud. Then my mom got sick and had to have liver surgery. I had to be there for her during that time, and I was very afraid. My whole family took a toll. Then the Lord healed my mother and she recovered just fine. All of this was right around my 19th birthday, and then I suddenly started to have massive headaches. Two weeks later I'm told I have a brain tumor and I undergo brain surgery with school on the back burner but still very much in my heart. I then get the results on the removed tumor: cancer. I go through radiation, chemo, all aggressive treatment. I lose lots of hair, go through post-traumatic stress and spiritual/emotional/physical/financial ups and downs, and to top it off, I tried to do the 2008 Fall semester at my old community college. I ended up having to drop out, though, because I was just too sick. I felt like a failure. I felt alone. I felt abnormal because I was 19 and out of school, sick in bed most of the time while my friends were all in school and "normal." The passion remained to be an SLP and to use my passions for writing, communication and therapy/service to others. I wrote a lot while the Lord had me to be taking a timeout on the sidelines. I finished a novel, began writing on another. I wrote songs, came up with ideas. I was bursting at the seams to be useful, to do something with my crazy imagination. Sometimes I felt worthless and useless to have a perfect GPA, membership in Phi Theta Kappa, a willingness to learn and apply myself, but no energy to physically go to school.

Enter 2009. I stopped treatment because the tumor was gone. My hair started coming back, my energy too. I was immediately thinking of school again, and pursued enrollment at the university. By now it was seeming like a far-off dream again. I mean, hey, they turned me away before, so why would they let up now? I was doubting it. But I gave it a shot, and lo and behold, the doors opened. I cried when I read that acceptance letter. I cried like a girl who'd just won the lottery. Then I went to Duke and the MRI showed tumor again. I cried when the doctor left the room, even though I didn't want my mom to see me do it. She said it would be okay and we came back home. I started taking oral chemo pills the next night, and I had an infusion at Duke after seeing my doctor. I kept thinking: "But I'm in school. They let me in! Remember, God? They let me in this time!" But I knew He was aware of this, and He's always up to something though I may not see it.

I've been throwing up, feeling nauseous, said farewell to my appetite (again) and bracing myself. The night before school, with all fees paid, backpack purchased, pencils sharpened, I was sick. I'd been through an emotional and physical whirlwind just from being back on chemo again - forget being told you've got cancer again. Treatment is a *beast*! And the chemo was making me vomit and feel miserable. That Sunday night before school, all I could do was cry and hope sleep would come. My dream was only hours away, class would start at 10:20, but Stephanie. was. out. I cried because, if I walked away, that meant my passion would be placed on hold . . . again. And I hated the thought of shooting myself in the foot.

Morning came. My alarm went off. I felt like a new person . . . well, sort of (you can only feel *so* much better when on chemo). I got up, showered, got dressed. Gathered my bags. My mom looked at me and asked me what I was doing. I said "I'm going to school, Mom."

I felt like an idiot, being a "new face" in an unfamiliar, new place—especially as a community college girl in a university (like going from country to city). Trying to remind myself that, no, it's *not* obvious to everyone I have a brain tumor and am getting chemo. (Talk about feeling self-conscious on your first day lol.) First class was Phonetics. Wow, this was real! The teacher *knows* what speech-language pathology is? You mean she actually gets it and teaches principles that SLPs need to know on the job? And these other students around me also share my desire to help those who struggle with communication? Wow. And to think I once felt I was all alone .

I did have to tell my teachers about my situation, and that part is always a bummer because I'm the type who *hates* excuses and I don't want anyone to pity me or doubt me. I just want to blow these classes out of the water like I did once upon a time. I want to be normal and compete with myself.

But finally, I have arrived to where I was trying to be all along. I may not know how at this moment as I type this, but my gifts and passions will not be wasted.

Welcome home, Steph. . .

5:26 P.M.

Sep 17, 2009

The last MRI looked much better, praise God. :) The doctor said it was about 75% better than before, and that the improvement was astounding because it happened so much in such a short time. Basically, I take that as God doing something in my brain. All of the glory, honor and credit for this goes to Him alone. Point-blank.

I was SO nervous before I got the results. Sitting in that room can drive you crazy, waiting for the doctor to come and give you the results. But the physician's assistant I had prior was such a blessing. I always see a PA before I see the doctor, and they run some psychological and physical tests just to see how I'm doing. She was a really nice lady this time, and she joked that I needed to relax when she checked my heartbeat (it's ALWAYS racing before I get the results). So that was a good laugh to have. I wonder if some of these people know how much they are helping patients when they do small things, simple things like just telling a joke— making you smile.

Anyway, I'll keep ahead with the same treatment, since it's working so well (thank the Lord). It makes me pretty sick, though. It's not easy. It also makes school a bit harder, especially since I missed two days while I was out of town. And I just noticed my hair coming out again . . . But you know what? I'm learning to be grateful and just live, breathe, emote, pray, act. I don't know if that makes any sense, but I'm done with having a mindset of this battle being the only thing about me, the only thing that's of any importance or what makes me interesting. I want to get back to my creativity, with actually SHARING it with you via this page.

I think there are times when I allowed myself to believe that Stephanie, as of summer of 2008, was only a girl fighting cancer, and nothing else. And it's still hard to fight that mindset, that thinking that I need to hide from people because I make them feel awkward or that I don't deserve happiness due to this struggle. But I've got a life to live, things to do, people to serve. God's given me that, so it's time for me to act like it and do as He says for me to do. If that means taking disgusting chemo, finishing this novel, losing my hair (again), and somehow juggling school in there, then I'm game!
12:33 A.M.

Oct 14, 2009

Prayer Request for my hand

Current mood: :) thankful

My left arm and hand/finger have weakened over the past few weeks. There's a slowness to my finger movement and it's hard to type, hold things, etc. I'm a classically trained pianist, so it's still very weird to be sending messages to my fingers to move quickly and they just kind of don't. It's like moving underwater and a loss of dexterity. It's also frustrating because I can't type notes on my netbook in class anymore, and as you can imagine, piano and guitar are no-no's.

You all know me; my hobbies revolve around my hand - at least the manifestation of them does. So writing has been almost at a standstill, and I mean on the story/novel, mainly. I knew something was wrong when I couldn't play my guitar one morning . . . . . . What did the docs say? Well, it's probably from brain swelling, b/c the MRI they ordered about a week ago didn't really show a change that would point to tumor growth. So I'm on steroids to help this get better, and I'm waiting to hear if physical therapy could also be an option.
School is going well, somehow I'm making A's (praise God for sure). I feel fine physically, the nausea's been pretty controlled and I did much better with this latest round of chemo. I just had an infusion today, and I'm taking a break on the nightly chemo pills before I start the next cycle, then it's back to Duke in November for another scan.
My nausea was going up and down for a while, and you can imagine the frustration with typing (I'm basically using my right hand only when on a computer) so that's why it's taken me so long to post this.

I'll keep you updated. Thank you.   2:43 A.M.

AFTERWORD

An Invitation to Heaven

"For God so loved the world that he gave his one and only Son, that whoever believes in Him shall not perish but have eternal life."

John 3:16

If you don't know Jesus; if you have never accepted Jesus Christ as your personal Lord and Savior, and you truly come to a saving faith and belief in Jesus and repent of your sins, you can pray a simple prayer as Stephanie references in her testimony at the beginning of this book.

"Heavenly Father, I have sinned. I am sorry and I repent. I believe that your Son Jesus Christ died on the cross to save me from my sins, arose from the dead and ascended into heaven. Jesus, please come into my heart as my personal Lord and Savior."

You can be assured that you will see Jesus face-to-face, in heaven, just as Stephanie is doing right now.

D.B.

Notes

High School Graduation Speech, page 101:

Williamson, Marianne. A Return to Love: *Reflections on the Principles of "A Course in Miracles."* New York: Harper Collins, 1992. Print.

44925789R00075